NHK NEWSLINE 3

Tatsuroh Yamazaki
Stella M. Yamazaki

KINSEIDO

Kinseido Publishing Co., Ltd.
3-21 Kanda Jimbo-cho, Chiyoda-ku,
Tokyo 101-0051, Japan

First published 2020 by Kinseido Publishing Co., Ltd.

Video materials NHK (Japan Broadcasting Corporation)

Authors and publisher are grateful to NHK Global Media Services, Inc. and all the interviewees who appeared on the news.

はじめに

NHK 英語放送を利用したこのシリーズが刊行されてから、今回で 25 冊目の出版を迎えることができた。これも皆様のご愛顧ご支援のおかげであり、心より感謝申し上げる。

いよいよ今年は東京五輪の年。都の試算では会期中の累計来場者は全国各地や世界中から約 1,564 万人と見込まれている。リンガフランカ（国際共通語）として英語が国内で使用される機会が日本史上最大に膨れ上がることは歴然としている。

これから、特に若い人にとって英語コミュニケーション力はまったなしである。さらに大学入学共通テストでは、2024 年に導入が考慮されている民間の資格・検定試験が、4 技能評価に適合するものとして活用される予定である。すでに多くの大学で推薦入試や AO 入試などでも 4 技能を見る英語試験が増えている実情がある。

アウトプット技能は、インプット技能と別物ではなく表裏一体の関係にある。会話で言うならば、「話す」技能はその基礎に「聞く」技能が前提とされるということである。どんな表現が通じるしぜんな英語なのかを聞き取り、（文字を通すなどして）それを覚えれば、すぐに自分の英語の表現の一部として発話できるのである。そういう意味でこれからますます、リスニングの重要性が強調されていくことになるであろう。

会話は音声のインプットとアウトプットの合わせ技だが、外国語は徹底的に聞いて模倣するという姿勢が常に必要である。従って伝統的な反復練習や文型練習は、語学学習者にとって必須である。目で追うだけではなく何回か反復して「音読」しておこう。音読しておけば記憶に定着しやすく、会話でもとっさのときに出てくるという利点がある。学習者にとって外国語の会話は（運動競技と同様に）スキルであり、練習によって積み上げた「記憶」が頼りなのである。

本書はリスニングを中心課題に据えたニュースの視聴覚教材である。映像は NHK 海外向け放送の NEWSLINE から採択し、適切な長さに編集した。この番組は現代日本の主なできごとや経済、文化、科学の最近の動向などを簡潔にまとめており好評を博している。

語学は授業中の学習だけではじゅうぶんではない。本書のニュース映像はオンラインで視聴可能なので、自宅で納得いくまで見てほしい。その際、まず完成したスクリプト（News Story の穴埋め問題終了後）を見ながら音声と意味の対応を頭に入れ、その後は文字を見ないで聞くという作業が必要である。この繰り返しが何回かあれば、文字なしで映像音声の理解ができるという快感が味わえるようになる。

末筆ながら、本書の作成に関して金星堂編集部をはじめ関係スタッフの方々に大変お世話になった。さらに出版にあたって NHK、株式会社 NHK グローバルメディアサービスの皆様にも映像提供などでご協力をいただいた。ここに厚くお礼を申し上げる。

2020 年 1 月　　編著者　山﨑達朗／ Stella M. Yamazaki

本書の構成とねらい

本書は全部で 15 単元（units）からなり、各単元とも、①日本語のイントロダクション、② Words & Phrases、③ Before You Watch、④ Watch the News、⑤ Understand the News、⑥ News Story、⑦ Review the Key Expressions、⑧ Discussion Questions という構成になっている。このうち①と②は説明で、③〜⑧が練習問題である。

① 日本語のイントロダクション

この短い日本語の説明（140 語前後）は、ニュースの要点を把握することを目的としている。外国語のリスニングには、何がどのように飛び出してくるかわからないという緊張と不安が常に伴うので、このように限られた背景知識（background knowledge）でも、予め準備があると安心感が出るものである。

② Words & Phrases

比較的難しいか、カギになる語彙や熟語などを学習する。ここで意味的、文法的知識をつけておけば、ニュースを聞いた場合に戸惑いは少なくなる。必要に応じて簡単な例文も入れてある。

③ Before You Watch

ニュース映像を見る前に、その予備知識を獲得したり話題を膨らませたりする意味で単元ごとに違った課題が用意してある。内容としては、日常会話表現の学習であったり、社会・文化に特有な語彙を英語でどう言うかといった課題であったりする。方法としても活動に興味が持てるように、ややゲーム的な要素も入れるようにしてある。英語の語彙を縦横に並んだアルファベット表から見つけ出すタスクや、クロスワードの活用もその例である。

④ Watch the News — First Viewing

ここで初めてクラスで映像を見るわけだが、課題はニュース内容の大きな流れや要点の理解が主となる基本的把握である。設問が3つあり、各問とも内容に合っていればT（= True)、合っていなければF（= False）を選択し、問題文の真偽を判断する。外国語のリスニングはしぜんに耳から入ってくるということがないので、集中して聞く必要がある。必要に応じて随時、<u>視聴の回数を増やしたり、問題と関連する箇所を教師が集中的に見せたり</u>するということが過去の経験から有効である。

⑤ Understand the News — Second Viewing

同じニュース映像をもう一度見るが、内容についてのやや詳細な質問となっている。次の２種類の下位区分がある。ここも必要に応じ、複数回のリスニングを考慮してほしい。

1 最初の視聴と比べて今度は選択肢が３つになっており、内容もより詳細にわたる設問が用意してある。各問、右端の３枚の写真は、参考にはなるが、問題を解く上でリスニングのキーとなる部分の映像とは限らないので注意してほしい。

2 単元によって、何種類か様々な形式の設問が用意してある。いずれもニュース内容や単語の用法の確認を目的としている。例えばニュースのまとめとなる「概要」や「入手情報の順序づけ」、要点となる数字の記入などである。さらに、設問によっては、ややゲーム的な要素を考慮し、アルファベットの並べ替え（unscrambling）を入れている。

⑥ News Story

これはニュース映像に対応するスクリプトであるが、完全なものにするには「穴埋め問題」を解く必要がある。問題は合計７問で、各問題に６箇所位の空所がある。解答するには、スタジオでややゆっくり読まれた音声CDをクラスで（各２回繰り返し）聞きながら書き取り作業（dictation）をする。スクリプトのそれぞれの問題には、右端におおまかな日本語訳（数字以外）がつけてあるのでヒントになる。書き取りが完成すればニュース映像の全文が目で確かめられるが、スクリプトは映像を見る前に読むことはせず、まず何回か視聴して上記④と⑤の設問に解答した後に、この穴埋めに挑戦してほしい。

⑦ Review the Key Expressions

ここでは、映像で出てきた単語や熟語などのうち応用性のある表現に習熟することがねらいである。そのような重要表現の意味や用法を確実にするとともに、英作文があまり負担なく身につくように単語を与える「整序問題」形式（４問）を採用した。ただし選択肢の中に錯乱肢（distractors）を１語入れ、適度に難しくしてある。文例は当該単元の話題とは関係なく、いろいろな場面の設定になっている。

⑧ Discussion Questions

最後の問題として、クラス内での話し合いに使える話題を２つ用意してある。当該単元に関連した身近な話題が提示してあるので、短く簡単な英語で自分の考えを表現してみる、というのがねらいである。（ご指導の先生へ：クラスによっては宿題として、話すことを次回までに考えておくというスタンスでもよいと思われる。この話し合いの課題は、人数や時間などクラス設定との兼ね合いから、用途に応じて柔軟に扱うのがよいと考えられる。）

NHK NEWSLINE 3

Contents

UNIT 1 Gunning for Glory

クレー射撃親子
—— 東京五輪を狙え！

若きクレー射撃選手の折原梨花さんは東京五輪を目指して練習を続けてきた。国際大会での実績もあり、待望のニューヒロインとして注目されている。父の研二さんもクレー射撃の選手で、日本を代表する１人である。梨花さんは親子で五輪に出るのが夢で、厳しい練習にも音をあげず目標を一点に見すえている。

● Words & Phrases

CD 02

☐ **up-and-coming**　新進の、頭角をあらわした

☐ **hotshot**　有望選手

☐ **clay shooting**　クレー射撃〈空中に放出された標的（クレー）を散弾銃で射撃して、割れた数を競う〉

☐ to **emulate**　～を手本とする
The new CEO will be successful if she *emulates* the business style of her father.
新 CEO は、彼女の父のビジネススタイルを手本とするなら成功するだろう。

☐ to **down**　～を撃ち落とす

☐ **field of vision**　視野、視界

☐ **prestigious**　名声の高い、格上の、一流の
Sho was enrolled in a *prestigious* university in the U.S.
翔は米国の名門大学に入学した。

☐ **line of vision**　視線　　☐ to **tighten one's belt**　《略式》倹約する

☐ **gratitude**　感謝（の念）、謝意　　☐ **preliminary**　予選の

☐ **qualifier**　出場決定戦

☐ **skeet**　スキート射撃〈クレー射撃の一種で、左右から打ち上げられる標的を撃つ〉

Before You Watch

以下は、東京五輪競技などに関する語彙です。適切な単語を空所に入れましょう。頭文字（群）が与えてあるものもあります。

1. アーチェリー　(　　　　　　　　)
2. バドミントン　(　　　　　　　　)
3. マラソン　(　　　　　　　　)
4. 競歩　(**r**　　　　　　　　) walk
5. フェンシング　(　　　　　　　　)
6. 射撃　(　　　　　　　　)
7. トライアスロン　(　　　　　　　　)
8. 陸上ホッケー　(**f**　　　　　　　　) hockey
9. 水球　water (**p**　　　　　　　　)
10. 予選　(**pre**　　　　　　　　)
11. 準々決勝　(**q**　　　　　　　　)
12. 準決勝　(**s**　　　　　　　　)
13. 決勝　(**f**　　　　　　　　)
14. 金メダル　(　　　　　　　　) medal
15. 銀メダル　(　　　　　　　　) medal
16. 銅メダル　(　　　　　　　　) medal

Watch the News

First Viewing

ニュースを見て、内容と合っているものは T、違っているものは F を選びましょう。

1. Rika Orihara won a junior world championship last year. [T / F]
2. Kenji won the All Japan's Championships many years consecutively. [T / F]
3. During the preliminary qualifier, Rika was ahead of Ishihara. [T / F]

Understand the News　Second Viewing

1 ニュースをもう一度見て、各問の空所に入る適切な選択肢を a～c から選びましょう。

1. Kenji started clay shooting ____.
- **a.** when he was about 12 years of age
- **b.** at a later age than Rika did
- **c.** after it became an Olympic event

2. To make their field of vision wider, Kenji and Rika ____.
- **a.** toss and catch two balls without looking at them
- **b.** dribble two soccer balls in a straight line
- **c.** bounce two tennis balls, one with each hand

3. In the preliminary competition Rika ____.
- **a.** scored less than 100 points
- **b.** downed 125 clay targets
- **c.** finished four points behind

2 以下はニュースの概要です。空所に適切な単語を書き入れましょう。語頭の文字（群）は与えてあります。

Rika Orihara is 21 years old and a senior at (**u** 1). She is a prospective clay shooting champion. She won last year's (**j** 2) category world competition. Her father, Kenji, is a top player and has won (**pr** 3) championships many times. Kenji advises Rika about shooting (**te** 4). They practice hard and are trying to both (**m** 5) it to the Tokyo Olympics. Rika joined the preliminary competition to help qualify for the Olympics but wound up in (**s** 6) place. She decided to work harder to show her (**gr** 7) to Kenji.

3 CD の音声を聞いて、次ページ News Story の❶～❼の文中にある空所に適切な単語を書き入れましょう。音声は２回繰り返されます。 CD 03

● News Story

Narrator: One **up-and-coming hotshot** in **clay shooting** is 21-year-old Rika Orihara.

Rika Orihara (Clay skeet shooter): Clay shooting is really fun. I enjoy it a lot.

Narrator: Rika's father, Kenji, is one of the sport's top players.

Rika: We're aiming high. For me, to make it to the Olympics. And if possible, to compete on that stage with my dad.

Narrator: ❶ Rika is ([1]) ([2]) ([3]) ([4]) ([5]) ([6]). She started clay shooting three years ago. Rika may be a new face on the scene, but she's already made a mark, winning last year's world championships in the junior category. Now she's looking to **emulate** her father's shooting style.

Kenji is known for his speed, quickly **downing** each target after it's released. He's trained himself to have a wider **field of vision**, helping reduce the time he needs to take aim.

Kenji started clay shooting when he was 24. He won the **prestigious** All Japan Clay Shooting Championships seven times in a row. ❷ Now with the Tokyo Olympics in sight, ([1]) ([2]) ([3]) ([4]) ([5]) ([6]) Rika.

(*Rika and Kenji are playing catch using two balls.*) This exercise develops a wider field of vision. By focusing on her father, not the balls, Rika should be able to shoot without shifting her **line of vision**.

It's a costly sport. ❸ ([1]) ([2]) ([3]) ([4]) ([5])

❶ 大学の最高［最終の］学年で

❷ 彼は～に自分の技術を伝えている

❸ それぞれの練習セッションは～発の射撃からなる

([6]). To some people, that's 60 dollars up in smoke. But not for Kenji and his daughter. The financial demands mean they **tighten their belts** elsewhere.

Kenji Orihara: I cook whenever I'm at home. ❹ And also ([1]) ([2]) ([3]) ([4]) ([5]).

❹ 練習（目的の）旅行のとき（も）

Narrator: ❺ Rika hopes to repay her father by ([1]) ([2]) ([3]) ([4]) ([5]) ([6]).

❺ 一流の射手ということを証明すること

Rika: The best way to show my **gratitude** is to produce results. ❻ That ([1]) ([2]) ([3]) ([4]) ([5]) ([6]).

❻ 私の父を本当に喜ばせるでしょう

Narrator: Rika took part in a **preliminary qualifier** for the world championships. It's an important stepping stone towards making it to the Olympics. She aims to compete in the women's **skeet** category of the 2020 games.

The final round. Rika tries to close the gap. The result: Ishihara finishes with 105 points out of 125 and Orihara has 101 for second place.

Rika: Well, I tried my best, but it just wasn't good enough. I made lots of errors. ❼ I'll ([1]) ([2]) ([3]) ([4]) ([5]) ([6]) . He's already told me I need to work harder.

❼ 父を喜ばせるように練習を続けます

Narrator: Rika and her father hope their shot *of** the Olympics will be on target.

Note

＊ここは forが正しい

Review the Key Expressions

各問、選択肢から適切な単語を選び、英文を完成させましょう。なお、余分な単語が１語ずつあります。

1. 山の天気が突然変わって、登山者たちは山小屋まで戻れる［～ができる］かどうか心配した。

The ( ) on the ( ) changed suddenly, and the climbers ( ) ( ) they would ( ) ( ) back to their hut.

it wondered mountain make weather happened if

2. 夫妻ともあまり収入がないので、時々節約しなければならない。

The husband and his wife do not ( ) much ( ), so they ( ) to ( ) their ( ) from time to ( ).

belts money often have time tighten make

3. 中国による政府抑圧に反対する集団デモのグループに加わったことで、多くの香港の学生が逮捕された。

Many students in Hong Kong were ( ) for ( ) ( ) in a ( ) demonstration ( ) government ( ) by China.

against arrested control taking group role part

4. 英語プレゼンのクラスで、よい学生はトップの成績をとろうといつもベストを尽くす。

Good students always ( ) ( ) ( ) to ( ) top ( ) in the English ( ) course.

grades present their best presentation try get

● Discussion Questions

1. What events are you most interested in at the 2020 Tokyo Olympic Games? Why?

2. Which do you like better: team sports like baseball, or individual sports like marathons? Why?

UNIT 2

Video Bingeing

進化する料理動画

今、ネット上で人気の動画がある。料理のレシピをわかりやすく短時間で紹介する映像なのだが、誰でもおいしく簡単に作れる料理法を配信するというのが売りで、撮影の角度や時間制限の工夫がなされ好評である。この動画のスーパーでの利用や、食品会社のクーポンと組み合わせた販売戦略が実験されている。

● Words & Phrases

CD 04

□ to **binge**　（過度に）熱中する、ふける〈cf. binge on sweets 甘いものを大食いする〉

□ **rage**　大流行、大人気

□ to **feast**　大いに楽しむ〈on を伴う〉　　□ **ingredient**　要素、条件；材料

□ to **whip up**　〈料理など〉を手早く作る
Shiori *whipped up* a salad for us.
詩織は私たちのためにサラダを手早く作ってくれた。

□ to **tempt**　（人）を（～に）引き付ける

□ **bite-size**　《口語》簡単に理解できる〈「一口大の」が原義〉

□ **hand**　人手

□ to **draw on**　～に頼る、～を利用する

□ to **bring ... to life**　～を生き生きさせる

□ to **pitch**　《口語》～を売り込む
He was in charge of *pitching* his company's freeze-dried foods at the sales convention.　彼は販売促進会で、自社のフリーズドライ食品の宣伝担当だった。

□ **app**　アプリ　　□ to **redeem**　〈クーポンなど〉を商品に換える

□ **payoff**　利益、もうけ　　□ **punch**　《口語》効果、パンチ

Before You Watch

以下は、料理に関する表現です。適切な単語を空所に入れましょう。なお、余分な単語もあります。

1. キャベツを千切りにする　to (　　　　) cabbage
2. 野菜を炒める　to (　　　　) vegetables
3. タマネギを揚げる　to (　　　　) onions
4. ニンジンの皮をむく　to (　　　　) carrots
5. 肉を解凍する　to (　　　　) meat
6. シャンパンを冷やす　to (　　　　) champagne
7. チーズをおろす　to (　　　　) cheese
8. 生地をこねる　to (　　　　) dough
9. 塩ひとつまみ　a (　　　　) of salt
10. 料理の材料　(　　　　)

11. フライパン　(　　　　) pan
12. ヘラ　(　　　　)
13. ざる　(　　　　)
14. 電動泡立て器　(　　　　)
15. 中華鍋　(　　　　)
16. 電子レンジ　(　　　　) oven
17. おたま　(　　　　)
18. 小さじ　(　　　　)
19. 大さじ　(　　　　)
20. （食器用）ふきん　(　　　　)

broiler	chill	cooker	deep-fry	defrost	dishcloth	frying	freeze
grate	ingredients	knead	ladle	microwave	mixer	peel	pinch
shred	simmer	spatula	stir-fry	strainer	tablespoon	teaspoon	wok

Watch the News

First Viewing

ニュースを見て、内容と合っているものは T、違っているものは F を選びましょう。

1. Speed in preparing recipes is an important feature of cooking videos. [T / F]
2. The recipe videos were made by a group of famous cooks. [T / F]
3. The food company is happy to receive data from customers. [T / F]

Understand the News　Second Viewing

1 ニュースをもう一度見て、各問の空所に入る適切な選択肢を a ～ c から選びましょう。

1. Due to the recipe videos, the store has sold ____ times as many of the promoted goods.
a. two
b. three
c. ten

2. The people making the videos chose from ____ recipes.
a. nearly three million
b. a little over four million
c. about two billion

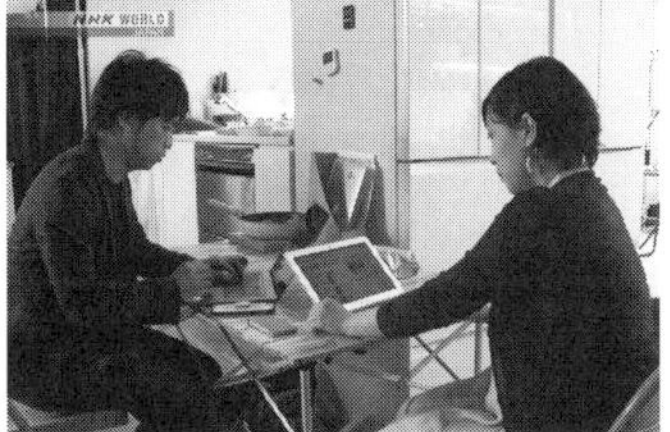

3. To receive the points from the coupon, you have to ____.
a. take it to the store and buy promoted foods
b. send a photo of your receipt to the video company
c. just wait one week for the store to process it

2 右の文字列を並べ替えて単語を作り、各文の空所に入れて意味がとおるようにしましょう。語頭の文字（群）が与えてあるものもあります。

1. Hokuto used to bake pastries as a hobby, but it's a (**se**) business for him now. [rosui]
2. On rainy days the store hardly attracts any (**c**).〈複数形〉 [mustores]
3. In ( ) to being a good mother, Hina is an excellent teacher. [anotdidi]
4. Try to collect as much (**in**) as possible before you visit a country. [mainofotr]

3 CD の音声を聞いて、次ページ News Story の❶～❼の文中にある空所に適切な単語を書き入れましょう。音声は２回繰り返されます。 CD 05

● News Story

Anchor: Cooking videos are all the **rage** on social media sites. Facebook and Instagram users are **feasting** on the snappy recipe guides, and a fast-growing business in Japan is profiting from the trend. NHK World's Jenny Lin reports.

Narrator: The key **ingredient** is speed. ❶ Cooking videos **whip up** mouthwatering dishes ([1]) ([2]) ([3]) ([4]) ([5]). Done right, they're informative and fun.

❶ 〜秒以内で

What started as Internet diversion is now serious business. ❷ ([1]) ([2]) ([3]) ([4]) ([5]) ([6]), a supermarket is using recipe videos to **tempt** customers.

❷ 野菜と鮮魚コーナーでは

The **bite-size** marketing tools seem to be working. Sales of promoted items have doubled since the monitors were installed.

The videos were produced by a recipe website operator. The entire operation—directors, camera operators and kitchen **hands**—is dedicated to making cooking programs.

❸ In making the videos, they ([1]) ([2]) ([3]) ([4]) ([5]) ([6]) on the website. Staff can **draw on** the database of 2.8 million dishes. The idea is to **bring** supermarket ingredients **to life**.

❸ もっとも人気のあるレシピから選択する

Tomoyuki Honzawa (General Manager, Cookpad TV): ❹ To produce the videos, we select recipes ([1]) ([2]) ([3]) ([4]) ([5]). This is what we're good at.

❹ 私たちのウェブサイトユーザーに好まれている

Narrator: ❺ ([1]) ([2]) ([3]) ([4]) ([5]) ([6]) looking for a slice of the action. This cooking video maker is **pitching** an idea to a food manufacturer. It's offering to add

❺ 小売店だけが〜なのではない

coupons to the mix.

❻ This is the video **app** (　　　　[1]) (　　　　[2]) (　　　　[3]) (　　　　[4]) (　　　　[5]). The coupons appear when you watch a video. You then head to a supermarket to buy the ingredients. To **redeem** the coupon, you take a picture of the receipt and send it to the video company, and that earns you points.

❻ すべてのクーポンがついている

The **payoff** for the food company is data. It knows what you've purchased in addition to its own products.

Daisuke Sekimoto (Mizkan): This data can be integrated *in** our marketing strategy.

Narrator: Coupons and cooking videos: The video distributor claims it all adds up to a powerful sales **punch**.

Taisei Yoshida (CEO, Every): By gathering information on our users' shopping at stores, and organizing it into an online database for our sponsors to access, we can contribute to making a big change in marketing at companies.

Narrator: ❼ (　　　　[1]) (　　　　[2]) (　　　　[3]) (　　　　[4]) (　　　　[5]) (　　　　[6]), but they're promising more value to come. Jenny Lin, NHK World.

❼ 動画制作者たちはまだ実験中である

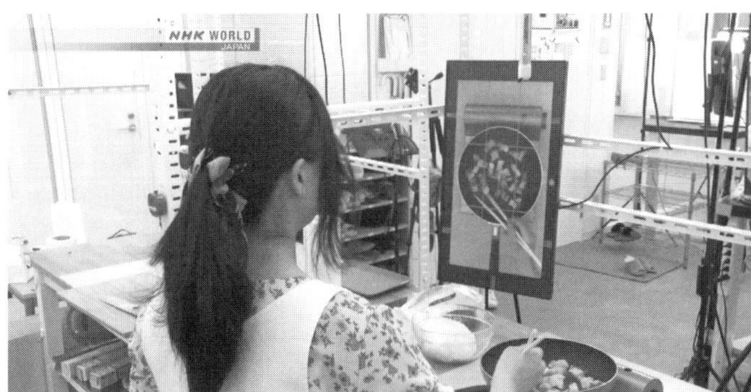

Note

* into のほうがよい

Review the Key Expressions

各問、選択肢から適切な単語を選び、英文を完成させましょう。なお、余分な単語が 1 語ずつあります。

1. 出前をとる必要はないよ。数分あればサンドウィッチをさっと作るから。

There is no (　　　　　) to (　　　　　) out. Just (　　　　　) me a (　　　　　) minutes to (　　　　　) (　　　　　) some sandwiches.

give　up　need　few　hold　whip　order

2. 新しい技術が導入されてから、会社の利益は倍増した。

(　　　　　) (　　　　　) have (　　　　　) since the (　　　　　) (　　　　　) was (　　　　　).

introduced　new　company　tripled　doubled　technology　profits

3. 若い社長の革新的な取り組みが本当に、業績の振るわない会社の息を吹き返させた。

The young president's (　　　　　) (　　　　　) really (　　　　　) his (　　　　　) company back (　　　　　) (　　　　　).

ailing　to　approach　life　brought　innovative　conservative

4. ジョージはチームに必要だと思うよ、私たちの得点に本当にかなり貢献しているからね。

I think we (　　　　　) (　　　　　) George on the team (　　　　　) he really (　　　　　) a (　　　　　) to (　　　　　) scores.

much　lot　should　our　because　keep　contributes

● Discussion Questions

1. Are you interested in cooking your own food? What are some advantages and disadvantages?

2. What kind of online videos or anime do you like best? Why?

UNIT 3 Speaking Their Language

外国人観光客と災害予知情報

日本は地震、豪雨、台風と自然災害の多い国である。近年外国人観光客が急増しているが、彼らは災害時に「情報難民」となり戸惑うことも多い。政府が観光立国を目標に掲げる一方で、そうした訪日客らに情報をどう速く正確に伝えるか、まだまだ整備されていない実情がある。あるユースホステルの対応の様子を紹介する。

● Words & Phrases

CD 06

☐ **natural disaster**　自然災害

☐ **vulnerable**　〈被害などを〉受けやすい
People with high blood pressure are *vulnerable* to strokes.
血圧の高い人は脳卒中を起こしやすい。

☐ **hostel**　ユースホステル、（青年旅行者用の）宿泊所

☐ to **spread the word**　ニュースを広める

☐ to **make landfall**　上陸する

☐ **in real time**　即時に、リアルタイムで
The freeway traffic information was reported *in real time*.
高速道路の交通情報がリアルタイムで報じられた。

☐ to **disrupt**　～を混乱させる、中断させる
The car accident *disrupted* rush hour traffic.
車の事故がラッシュアワーの道路［交通］を混乱させた。

☐ **million**　100 万〈cf. billion は 10 億、trillion は 1 兆〉

☐ **extravaganza**　豪華な催し

Before You Watch

以下は、旅行や買い物で使う表現です。下の枠内から適切な単語を選び、空所に入れましょう。

1. 観光案内所へ行きたいのですが。
Where can I find the tourist (   ) center?

2. どこでタクシーに乗れるでしょうか。
Could you tell me (   ) I can get a taxi?

3. 次の信号を右折すると、左手にその建物が見えてきます。
(   ) right at the next (   ) and you'll see the building on your left.

4. そのホテルまで、どのくらい時間がかかりますか。
How (   ) does it (   ) to get to the hotel?

5. 《ホテルで》数時間、スーツケースを預かっていただけますか。
Could you (   ) these suitcases for me for a few hours?

6. 午後６時ごろに戻ってきます。 I'll be (   ) at (   ) 6 p.m.

7. 《レストランへの電話》今晩３名の予約をお願いしたいのですが。
I'd like to (   ) a (   ) for three for tonight.

8. 何がお勧めですか。 What do you (   )?

9. 会計は別々にしていただけますか。 Could we have (   ) checks?

10. もう一度言っていただけますか。 Could you (   ) that again?

around	back	hold	information	long	make	recommend
reservation	say	separate	signal	take	turn	where

Watch the News — First Viewing

ニュースを見て、内容と合っているものはＴ、違っているものはＦを選びましょう。

1. The first tourist interviewed said he would need shelter the most. [T / F]

2. Travelers to Japan really need information in a language they can understand. [T / F]

3. In this hostel a dinner party was held for visitors. [T / F]

Understand the News　Second Viewing

1 ニュースをもう一度見て、各問の空所に入る適切な選択肢をａ～ｃから選びましょう。

1. According to the first woman interviewed, ____.
  a. staying at Japanese hotels is very expensive
  b. earthquakes don't really occur in European countries
  c. in Europe, public transport systems are rarely disrupted

2. In this youth hostel, they advised ____.
  a. foreigners to come back to Japan and enjoy hospitality
  b. foreign visitors to learn Japanese for better communication
  c. customers to change their schedules due to weather conditions

3. About ____ foreigners came to Japan last year.
  a. 2,800,000
  b. 28,000,000
  c. 280,000,000

2 右の文字列を並べ替えて単語を作り、各文の空所に入れて意味がとおるようにしましょう。語頭の文字が与えてあるものもあります。

1. Landslides and volcanic eruptions are examples of natural (　　　　　　　). 〈複数形〉 [stressaid]

2. The two international groups could not communicate well due to language (**b**　　　　　　　). 〈複数形〉 [resarri]

3. During Golden Week there were a lot of (**t**　　　　　　　) jams across Japan. [fiarcf]

4. Travelers should stay (**i**　　　　　　　) when typhoons make landfall in their area. [dnorso]

3 CD の音声を聞いて、次ページ News Story の❶～❼の文中にある空所に適切な単語を書き入れましょう。音声は２回繰り返されます。 CD 07

● News Story

Anchor: ❶ When **natural disasters** strike, as they have in Japan recently, some of the most **vulnerable** people are ([1]) ([2]) ([3]) ([4]) ([5]) ([6]). Last month as typhoon Charmy approached, a **hostel** in Osaka made sure its guests knew what was coming and what to do. NHK World's Kazuo Tatehata reports.

Narrator: We asked visitors to Japan what they thought their biggest problem would be in a disaster.

Man: I think information, because most of the information was in Japanese.

Woman: Europe, there's, there's no real like big... the typhoons don't really happen; earthquakes don't really happen. ❷ So, ([1]) ([2]) ([3]) ([4]) ([5]) ([6]).

Narrator: This hostel in central Osaka started **spreading the word** the day before the typhoon **made landfall**.

Shuhei Fujii: *I just want you to know ... that typhoon is coming tomorrow, and the day after tomorrow it's going to be at Osaka and Tokyo.**1

Foreign traveler: Trains like Shinkansen will be influenced by the typhoon?

Fujii: Yes, it depends on the JR company, so....

We were concerned by the language barrier, so we tried to provide as much information as possible **in real time**.

Narrator: Planes, trains and other forms of public transport have been seriously **disrupted** several times this year. ❸ ([1]) ([2]) ([3]) ([4]) ([5]) ([6]) they could understand.

❶ そのことば［言語］を話さない人たち

❷ みんな、どうしたらいいかわからない

❸ 多くの旅行者は、ぜひ情報がほしかった

The hostel prepared a list of the traffic and train problem[s]*[2].

Masahiro Ashida: ❹ I wanted them to understand that the typhoon was big enough to stop train services and that ([1]) ([2]) ([3]) ([4]) ([5]) ([6]).

❹（今）いるところに留まるべき

Narrator: ❺ ([1]) ([2]) ([3]) ([4]) ([5]), the hostel asked guests going out where they were headed. In some cases, it advised them to change their plans.

❺ 台風が接近してきた（状況で）

Ashida: Staying indoors would be best, but then again, since they are tourists, their time may be limited. We try to suggest good plans, considering the conditions.

Narrator: The typhoon was about to make landfall. Preparations were underway for a dinner party for overnight guests.

Mako Sakamoto: We wanted to do something for them because going out would have been difficult.

Narrator: ❻ ([1]) ([2]) ([3]) ([4]) ([5]) ([6]), they were less likely to put themselves at risk in the heavy rain and the strong wind.

❻ お客さんがもてなされていれば

Female traveler: She*[3] told me I shouldn't go too far and what time it's best to come back again. So it was fine. Yes.

Narrator: Twenty-eight **million** visitors from overseas came to Japan last year. That number is expected to grow with the staging of the Olympics in 2020. ❼ Of all the events connected with that **extravaganza**, disaster readiness ([1]) ([2]) ([3]) ([4]) ([5]) ([6]) ([7]). Kazuo Tatehata, NHK World, Osaka.

❼ すべてのことの中で、もっとも大切かもしれない

Notes

*[1] 音声が小さく不明瞭な部分が多いので、ここのスクリプトは推測に基づいた

*[2] 語末に -s が必要

*[3] She はホステルの女性スタッフをさす

Review the Key Expressions

各問、選択肢から適切な単語を選び、英文を完成させましょう。なお、余分な単語が 1 語ずつあります。

1. 私は「天は自ら助くる者［〜する人々］を助く」ということわざを強く信じている。

I ( ) believe the ( ) "( ) helps ( ) ( ) help ( )."

themselves those firmly myself Heaven who proverb

2. そのスポーツ講師は、激しい運動をする前の準備運動（についてその重要性）を周知させている。

The sports ( ) is ( ) the ( ) about ( ) up before ( ) strenuous ( ).

doing spreading warming letting exercise word instructor

3. 最終の成績は、すべて授業への参加と期末試験の結果による。

Your ( ) ( ) all ( ) ( ) your class ( ) and the ( ) of your final exam.

participation to final on grade depends result

4. 親友と大喧嘩してから、剛は彼からなるべく離れていようと決めた。

After having a big ( ) with his ( ) friend, Tsuyoshi decided to ( ) as ( ) away ( ) him ( ) possible.

as fight close stay far from not

● Discussion Questions

1. Have you ever gone through a natural disaster? What kind? What did you do?

2. Which countries or interesting places in Japan have you visited? Which did you enjoy most? Why?

UNIT 4 Creativity from the Campus

学生とコラボ

会社と大学が共同開発した商品が話題となっている。例えばフレッシュネスバーガーと立教大学の学生団体のコラボにより期間限定で商品化された「立教ごちそうバーガー」は女子学生をターゲットにし、おいしさやヘルシーさが売りである。若い世代の斬新なアイディアがいろいろな業種で期待される時代が来たようだ。

● Words & Phrases

CD 08

- ☐ **corporate**　法人の、会社の
- ☐ **headquarters**　本社
- ☐ to **tap**　～を開発する、利用する
- ☐ to **reach out to**　（人々）に接触しようとする
- ☐ **Genovese**　ジェノバ風の
- ☐ **ingenuity**　工夫、巧みさ
- ☐ to **come up with**　～を思いつく
  The owner of the apartment building *came up with* a solution to the tenant's noise problem.
  そのアパート（の建物）の所有者は、そのテナントの騒音問題の解決法を思いついた。
- ☐ to **tweak**　～を調整する
- ☐ **edgy**　《口語》かっこいい、最先端の
  The musician's songs are really *edgy*.
  そのミュージシャンの曲は本当にかっこいい。
- ☐ **harness**　ハーネス〈ロッククライミングの際に装着する安全ベルト〉
- ☐ to **bring ... to life**　～を生き生きさせる
- ☐ **boardroom**　理事［重役］会

Before You Watch

以下は、ファーストフード店と衣料品店で使う表現です。下の枠内から適切な単語を選び、空所に入れましょう。なお、余分な単語もあります。

1. こちら［店内で］お召し上がりですか、お持ち帰りですか。
For ( ), or to ( )?

2. 番号をお取りになって、テーブルでお待ちください。
( ) a number and wait at your table. Thank you.

3. このセットメニューはハンバーガー、お飲み物、それにフライドポテトになります。
This ( ) includes a hamburger, a drink and French ( ).

4. お並びですか。　Are you in ( )?

5. チーズバーガー２つとコーラのＬを２つください。
I'll take two cheeseburgers and two large ( ), please.

6. これ、試着してみていいですか。　Can I ( ) this ( )?

7. 試着室はどちらですか。　Where is the ( ) room?

8. このシャツ、色違いはありますか。
Do you carry the same shirt in ( ) colors?

9. 申し訳ありませんが、在庫がございません。
We're sorry, they are ( ) of ( ).

10. この（下着の）パンツはフリーサイズです。
These underpants are ( ).

all-you-can-eat	combo	Cokes	different	fitting	fries	go	here	in
line	on	one-size-fits-all	out	stock	take	there	try	waiting

Watch the News

First Viewing

ニュースを見て、内容と合っているものはＴ、違っているものはＦを選びましょう。

1. Rikkyo University actively looked for companies to work with. [T / F]
2. The hamburger the students created sold very well. [T / F]
3. Customers like the fashion designs the students made while working with Zara. [T / F]

Understand the News　Second Viewing

1 ニュースをもう一度見て、各問の空所に入る適切な選択肢をａ～ｃから選びましょう。

1. Manaka Susa explains that ____.
  a. Rikkyo burgers are not sold on campus
  b. she went to Genova to make their hamburgers
  c. the red cabbage in the dish stands for their school color

2. Zara ____.
  a. produced more than ten items designed by the students
  b. spent around four months looking for student designers
  c. had five students make a new climbing harness

3. These fast food and fast fashion producers in this report ____.
  a. are trying to set up more outlets in Tokyo
  b. will hire the student designers full-time
  c. were surprised at the students' ingenuity

2 右の文字列を並べ替えて単語を作り、各文の空所に入れて意味がとおるようにしましょう。語頭の文字（群）が与えてあるものもあります。

1. Some students together with a company, created the new (　　　　　　　). 〈複数形〉 [surgreb]
2. Rikkyo University is one of the (**l**　　　　　　　) universities in Japan. [gained]
3. Fashion brand Zara is headquartered in (**S**　　　　　　　). [npia]
4. Many people considered the students' design to be (**in**　　　　　　　). [avnoivet]

3 CD の音声を聞いて、次ページ News Story の❶～❼の文中にある空所に適切な単語を書き入れましょう。音声は２回繰り返されます。 CD 09

● News Story

Anchor: Businesses are constantly searching for the next big hit. Some companies operating in Japan are going outside their **corporate headquarters** to seek new ideas at places where creativity is just waiting to be **tapped**, on school campuses.

Clerk: This is the *Rikkyo University hamburger*.*1

Narrator: One of Japan's leading universities and a popular fast food chain came together to create this new burger. ❶ The chain was looking for (　　　1) (　　　2) (　　　3) (　　　4) (　　　5) (　　　6) to its restaurants and **reached out to** Rikkyo University.

❶ もっと多くの学生を引きつける方法

Manaka Susa (Rikkyo University): The red cabbage represents our school color. ❷ The ***Genovese****2 sauce symbolizes the ivy *covered**3 (　　　1) (　　　2) (　　　3) (　　　4) (　　　5) (　　　6).

❷ そのキャンパスの有名な壁

Narrator: One member of the chain's marketing team says she was surprised by the students' **ingenuity**.

Ibuki Kumagai (Freshness): ❸ We normally dwell on operational procedures and production costs (　　　1) (　　　2) (　　　3) (　　　4) (　　　5) (　　　6), but the students can set such factors aside and **come up with** *unique ideas**4.

❸ 私たちが新しいハンバーガー（の生産）を企画するとき

Narrator: The burger went on sale at an outlet near the university and became the top seller in no time.

Spanish fashion brand Zara came up with a similar idea recently. It teamed up with a Tokyo fashion college and produced 15 items designed by the students. It's the first time the global fast fashion leader has tried the idea.

Yuto Seki (Zara Roppongi Pop-up Shop): Some people are aware of the project and visit our shop to have a look. ❹ They ([1]) ([2]) ([3]) ([4]) ([5]) ([6]).

❹ その製品の背後にある物語が好きである

Narrator: Five students from Japan, France, Germany and Australia spent about four months designing the clothes. They **tweaked** a classical suit design to make it more **edgy**. It's decorated with orange strips modeled after a climbing **harness**.

Arashi Yunome (Bunka Gakuen University): The designs are simple. ❺ We tried to incorporate what we like into the designs, but it was difficult to ([1]) ([2]) ([3]) ([4]) ([5]) ([6]) at the same time.

❺ それら［デザイン］をシンプルにしながら、目立つようにする

Narrator: The students in Tokyo worked closely with designers and the Spanish head office to **bring** the designs **to life**.

Seki: ❻ They came up with ([1]) ([2]) ([3]) ([4]) ([5]) ([6]). ❼ Their ideas ([1]) ([2]) ([3]) ([4]) ([5]) ([6]). The designs are innovative. Customers like the products and think they're cool.

❻ 私たちが想像もしなかった新しいアイディア

❼ 私たちに、新しい製品を出させてくれた

Narrator: In fast food and fast fashion, the know-how of the **boardroom** and the ingenuity of the campus _has_*[5] proven to be a recipe for success.

Notes

＊[1] 現在、この商品は販売を終了している

＊[2] 語尾に -s の発音が聞こえるが、ここは形容詞なので Genovese のままが正しい

＊[3] colored という発音になっているが covered が正しい

＊[4] 直前に a の発音が聞こえるが、これは不要

＊[5] 文法的には have になる

Review the Key Expressions

各問、選択肢から適切な単語を選び、英文を完成させましょう。なお、余分な単語が 1 語ずつあります。

1. その兄弟は彼らの（意見の）相違に目をつぶって、一緒にビジネスを始めた。

The brothers (　　　　　) (　　　　　) their (　　　　　) and (　　　　　) (　　　　　) a new business (　　　　　).

opened　together　down　aside　set　differences　up

2. このシリーズの最新のテキストは毎年 1 月に発売される。

The (　　　　　) textbook in this (　　　　　) (　　　　　) (　　　　　) (　　　　　) in January (　　　　　) year.

goes　every　latest　on　series　final　sale

3. もう少しいらっしゃって、お昼をご一緒にいかがですか。サンドウィッチを 2、3 個とチリをすぐに作りますよ。

Why (　　　　　) you stay for lunch? I can make a (　　　　　) (　　　　　) sandwiches and a pot of chili (　　　　　) (　　　　　) (　　　　　).

no　don't　in　shortly　of　couple　time

4. パーティーに活気を与えるため、高志は自分のギターを弾き始め、お客さんたちに一緒に歌ってもらった。

To (　　　　　) the party (　　　　　) (　　　　　), Takashi started to play his guitar and (　　　　　) the guests to (　　　　　) (　　　　　).

along　bring　to　sing　live　got　life

● Discussion Questions

1. Do you like fast food? If you do, what kinds? If not, why not?

2. What kinds of clothes do you like to wear and what colors? Why?

UNIT 5

Firms Help Fight Plastic Pollution

日本企業の脱プラ対策

プラスチック製品は安価で軽量で丈夫な上、腐食もしない。しかしこれがいったんゴミになると、すべての利点が一気に汚染となって地球環境に襲いかかる。素材や加工技術の課題解決が急務となるなか、海の生態系を守りながら何がベストの解決法なのか、国連や各国首脳会合での討議は続く。

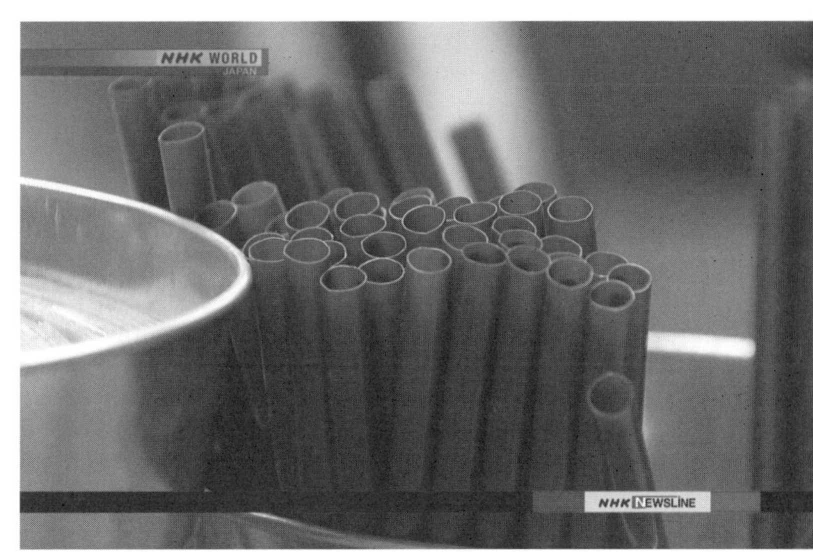

● Words & Phrases

CD 10

☐ to **step up**　向上する、立ち上がる
☐ **on one's own**　自分の判断で、独断で
☐ **proactively**　率先して　☐ to **throw out**　～を廃棄する
☐ **microorganism**　微生物　☐ **biodegradable**　微生物によって分解される
☐ to **accumulate**　～を蓄積する　☐ **start-up**　新設企業
☐ **no more ... than**　～と同様に…でない
I can *no more* hang glide *than* you can. Neither of us has had lessons.
君同様、僕もハンググライディングはまったくできない。２人とも訓練は受けていないからね。
☐ **limestone**　石灰岩　☐ **resin**　樹脂製品
☐ **fragile**　もろい　☐ **coral**　サンゴ
☐ to **crack down on**　《口語》～を厳しく取り締まる
☐ **second only to**　～に次いで２番目である
In our table tennis club, Hazuki is *second only to* Daiki at winning games.
私たちの卓球クラブで、葉月は大輝に次いで試合勝利数が多い。
☐ **per capita**　１人当たりの

Before You Watch

以下は、ごみ（処理）に関する語彙です。空所に適切な文字を入れ、下のクロスワードを完成させましょう。

ACROSS

1. 食品用プラスチックバッグ	plastic (**g** _ _ _ _ _ _) bag
2. プラスチック皿	plastic (_ _ _ _ _)
3. リサイクル可能な物〈複数形〉	(_ _ _ _ _ _ _ _ _ _ **s**)
4. (埋め立て式) ごみ処理場	(_ **an** _ _ _ _ _)
5. プラスチックごみ	plastic (**wa** _ _ _)
6. 生態系	(**ec** _ _ _ **s** _ _ _)
7. 使い捨てのプラスチック製品	(**s** _ _ _ _ _)-use plastic product

DOWN

8. プラスチックストロー	plastic (_ _ _ **a** _)
9. 環境に優しい	environmentally-(**f** _ _ _ **n** _ _ _)
10. 環境汚染	environmental (**p** _ _ _ _ _ _ _ _)
11. 環境保護の 3Rs	reduce, (**r** _ _ **s** _), recycle

Watch the News

First Viewing

ニュースを見て、内容と合っているものはT、違っているものはFを選びましょう。

1. There aren't any official restrictions against the use of plastics in Japan. [T / F]

2. The new plastic material which Mitsubishi Chemical Holdings developed is broken down in seawater. [T / F]

3. A start-up in Tokyo developed a plastic material, but it is a lot more expensive than conventional plastics. [T / F]

Understand the News　Second Viewing

1 ニュースをもう一度見て、各問の空所に入る適切な選択肢を a ～ c から選びましょう。

1. The new material Mitsubishi Chemical Holdings made is eaten by microorganisms in ____.
- **a.** a few days
- **b.** two months
- **c.** 30 years

2. The new material developed by Mitsubishi Chemical Holdings ____.
- **a.** did not require study
- **b.** takes advanced technology to produce
- **c.** is made from limestone and resin

3. The largest consumer of single use plastic is ____.

- **a.** Japan
- **b.** China
- **c.** the United States

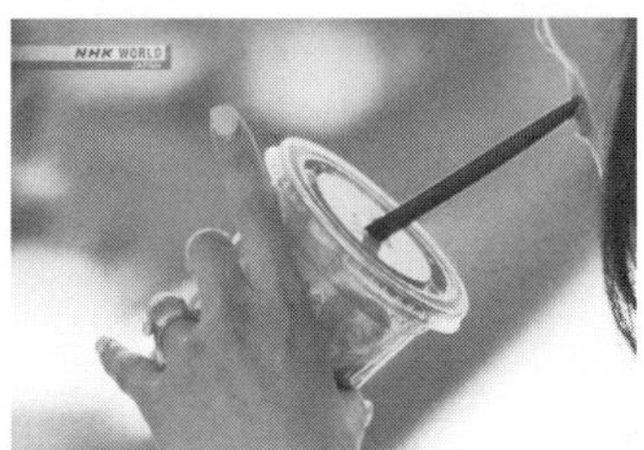

2 以下の各情報を、ニュースに出てきた順序に並べましょう。

1. The company has spent three decades developing biodegradable materials and the knowledge to use them.
2. Japan is one of the world's largest consumers of disposable plastic products.
3. Looking at the polluted sea prompts people to talk about limiting the use of plastics.
4. A Tokyo start-up company might have a solution: developing a cheaper biodegradable material.

3 CD の音声を聞いて、次ページ News Story の❶～❼の文中にある空所に適切な単語を書き入れましょう。音声は 2 回繰り返されます。　CD 11

● News Story

Narrator: It's scenes like this that are turning people against plastics and prompting talk of bans. In Japan there aren't any official restrictions yet, but companies are **stepping up** to address the issue **on their own**.

Tsutomu Tannowa** **(Chairman, Japan Initiative for Marine Environment): ❶ Japan can play a major role in improving management of plastic waste in countries and regions ([1]) ([2]) ([3]) ([4]) ([5]) ([6]). We'll work with the Japanese government and business groups that share this goal and **proactively** work on solving the problem.

❶ それを多く排出する［作り出す］～

Reporter** **(Tsukasa Uesugi): ❷ Some companies ([1]) ([2]) ([3]) ([4]) ([5]) ([6]). They see a way to profit on changing attitudes toward plastic by developing new materials, the type that won't damage the environment when they are **thrown out**.

❷ 業界の指針を待ってはいない

Narrator: Mitsubishi Chemical Holdings has come up with a material that's eaten by **microorganisms** in soil in just 60 days. If products wind up in the ocean, they'll be broken down by seawater.

❸ The ([1]) ([2]) ([3]) ([4]) ([5]) ([6]) developing **biodegradable** materials, **accumulating** patents and know-how.

❸（その）会社は～年以上費やした

And here's one of the results, used for everything from single use cups to more eco-friendly garbage bags.

Yoshihiro Fujimori** **(Division General Manager, Mitsubishi Chemical): It is a mission of the plastics industry to show people that plastics are developing in the right direction.

Narrator: ❹ But these materials ([1]) ([2]) ([3]) ([4]) ([5]) and ([6]), and require complex technology, all of which means a high price tag.

A **start-up** in Tokyo says it might have a solution. It's developing a biodegradable material that's **no more** expensive **than** conventional plastics. It's made from **limestone** and **resin** derived from plants. Place the material in soil at room temperature, and it starts breaking down in only a few days.

❺ Here's ([1]) ([2]) ([3]) ([4]) ([5]) ([6]). The sample on the far right is almost completely broken down, so it's very **fragile**. The only thing left is the limestone, which is pretty much the same as **coral**.

Nobuyoshi Yamasaki (CEO, TBM): Limestone is plentiful and cheap. Since it's our main ingredient, our costs go right down. Countries that don't even have a system in place to collect plastic waste are starting to **crack down on** plastic products. We want to help them by coming up with a fully biodegradable material.

Narrator: ❻ One industry leader says the efforts to fight plastic pollution ([1]) ([2]) ([3]) ([4]) ([5]).

Kotaro Kishimura (Executive Director, Japan Plastics Industry Federation): We should educate company employees so they get the big picture and that will lead them to create products or adopt business systems that don't damage the environment.

Narrator: Japan is one of the world's largest consumers of single use plastic. It's **second only to** the U.S. in **per capita** usage. ❼ But that may be about to change with ([1]) ([2]) ([3]) ([4]) ([5]) ([6]). Tsukasa Uesugi, NHK World.

❹ 多くの調査（と）開発を必要とする

❺ その物質が時間とともにどのように変化するか

❻ 新しいビジネスチャンスを生み出す

❼ いくつかの革新的な企業の協力

Review the Key Expressions

各問、選択肢から適切な単語を選び、英文を完成させましょう。なお、余分な単語が１語ずつあります。

1. 警察は、酒酔い運転を厳しく取り締まっており、より厳格な罰則を適用している。
The (   ) are (   ) (   ) on (   ) driving and (   ) stiffer (   ).

cracking　issuing　police　stepping　penalties　down　drunk

2. 米国では、日曜のスーパーボールは、感謝祭に次いで２番目に食料消費がもっとも盛んな日のひとつである。
In the U.S., Super Bowl Sunday (   ) as (   ) (   ) the country's biggest days for food (   ), (   ) only (   ) Thanksgiving Day.

one　to　second　of　consumption　except　ranks

3. 山形県は、１人あたりの年間ラーメン消費量が［～に関して］全国一多い。
In Japan, Yamagata Prefecture (   ) (   ) in (   ) of annual (   ) (   ) consumption of (   ).

ramen　ranks　capita　terms　per　about　first

4. 大事なことをしようとすると必ず（そのタイミングで）、なぜか彼女が助けを求めてくる。
(   ) she always (   ) my help (   ) I (   ) (   ) to do (   ) important.

whenever　somehow　about　must　am　something　needs

● Discussion Questions

1. Plastics are light, strong and cheap. Do you think we can keep using plastic products? Why?
2. Do you reuse or recycle things? If so, what do you do? If you don't, why not?

UNIT 6

Foreign Students Get Helping Hand

外国人留学生の就活

日本で就職する外国人が増加する中、留学生の就職活動を支援する会社が人気である。コーディネーターが個別指導でカウンセリングを行い、個別のニーズに合った企業や採用形態を仲介するサービスである。日本の社会や文化に不慣れな留学生と、受け入れる日本企業双方にとって、将来的にも重要な橋渡しとなる。

● Words & Phrases

CD 12

- ☐ **application form** 願書、申込用紙
- ☐ to **draw on** ～に頼る、～を生かす
- ☐ **contractor** 請負業者
- ☐ **in charge of** ～担当の、～係の
- ☐ **expertise** 専門技術
- ☐ **tip** 助言、ヒント
- ☐ **accounting** 会計学
- ☐ to **hail from** ～出身である
- ☐ to **lag behind** ぐずぐずして遅れる〈fall behind とも言う〉
- ☐ **keen** 熱心に～したくて
  Both companies are *keen* to reach an agreement.
  両方の会社ともお互いに合意したいと思っている。
- ☐ **with a view to** ～の目的で〈通例、名詞、動名詞を伴う〉
  He is studying hard *with a view to* becoming a doctor.
  彼は医者になろうと一生懸命に勉強している。
- ☐ **crucial** 非常に重要な、重大な

Before You Watch

以下は、国名・地名とその土地の人やことばを指す語彙です。空所に適切な単語を入れて完成させましょう。

Country/ City	People
e.g. Japan	(Japanese)
1. South Korea	South ( )
2. Vietnam	( )
3. Mongolia	( )
4. Taiwan	(**T**)
5. ( )	Filipino / Filipina
6. Nepal	( ) / Nepali
7. Afghanistan	( )
8. Brazil	( )
9. Peru	( )
10. Russia	( )
11. Germany	( )
12. ( )	French

Watch the News

First Viewing

ニュースを見て、内容と合っているものは T、違っているものは F を選びましょう。

1. Lim Seyoung is a South Korean born in Japan. [T / F]

2. Lim started a firm with a couple of Vietnamese two years ago. [T / F]

3. The Japanese government is trying to hire more foreigners. [T / F]

Understand the News　Second Viewing

1 ニュースをもう一度見て、各問の空所に入る適切な選択肢をａ～ｃから選びましょう。

1. Lim's company ____.
  a. provides information for Japanese about foreign language schools
  b. matches people who are looking for jobs with possible employers
  c. is located in the neighborhood of the business school she visited

2. The business school Lim visited ____.
  a. has 90 students from abroad
  b. has mostly foreign students
  c. only enrolls ten percent of new applicants

3. The second student from Nepal says that he ____.
  a. is going back to Nepal
  b. lost his job earlier
  c. is positive about finding a job

2 右の文字列を並べ替えて単語を作り、各文の空所に入れて意味がとおるようにしましょう。語頭の文字（群）が与えてあります。

1. I'm (**or**) from Fukuoka Prefecture, but I live in Tokyo now. [lilyaing]
2. The CEO is very (**ca**) and successfully opened three more branches last year. [lebap]
3. Every summer the village suffers from a (**sh**) of water. [geotra]
4. The (**de**) for health food has been increasing. [mdan]

3 CD の音声を聞いて、次ページ News Story の❶～❼の文中にある空所に適切な単語を書き入れましょう。音声は２回繰り返されます。 CD 13

● News Story

***Lim Seyoung* (Nasic I support):** (*She speaks Japanese on the phone.*) What about the student who hasn't found a job yet?

Narrator: Lim Seyoung is originally from Seoul. She came to Japan after graduating high school and studied the language before going on to university. Now she works at the firm that matches job seekers to potential employers. ❶ Lim knows all (　　　　[1]) (　　　　[2]) (　　　　[3]) (　　　　[4]) (　　　　[5]) (　　　　[6]) when looking for jobs in Japan.

❶ 外国人が直面する試練について

Seyoung: ❷ I didn't know how to do research on companies, (　　　　[1]) (　　　　[2]) (　　　　[3]) (　　　　[4]) (　　　　[5]) (　　　　[6]), or how to fill out **application forms**.

❷ どういう態度で面接を受けるか

Narrator: Lim **draws on** that experience to help others who are in a similar position. Two years ago, her firm placed two Vietnamese students at this electrical **contractor**. The company wants to expand into Southeast Asia and needs capable Vietnamese employees.

The recruits are already well-established at the firm and are now **in charge of** work schedules and safety. One of them recently received a high level engineering certification.

***Toshimichi Momma* (President, Shinko Electric):** ❸ We had no idea (　　　　[1]) (　　　　[2]) (　　　　[3]) (　　　　[4]) (　　　　[5]), but Lim's firm was able to provide exactly the **expertise** that we needed.

❸ 外国人の応募者をどのように引きつけるか

Narrator: Today Lim is visiting a business school near Tokyo to give **tips** to a group of **accounting** students. The number of foreigners at the school has been increasing rapidly. They now make up 90 percent of the students. The school has recently started helping them look for jobs.

Seyoung: Good afternoon, everyone.

Narrator: Many of the students **hail from** countries such as Vietnam, Nepal and Sri Lanka.

Seyoung: ❹ You only ([1]) ([2]) ([3]) ([4]) ([5]) ([6]), don't you? ❺ If so, please remember that you're part of the larger hiring picture, and by doing this, ([1]) ([2]) ([3]) ([4]) ([5]).

❹ 外国人学生向けのウェブサイトを調べる

❺ 自分の選択肢をかなり限定する

Student from Nepal (A): Now I understand that I have to put a lot of energy into finding work. ❻ And ([1]) ([2]) ([3]) thoroughly, ([4]) ([5]) ([6]).

❻ 準備しないと、うまくいかない

Student from Nepal (B): As long as I proceed step by step and don't **lag behind**, then I believe I can find a job.

Seyoung: ❼ I think it's important for me to ([1]) ([2]) ([3]) ([4]) ([5]) ([6]) and to continue helping them along the road towards finding work. I want more of them to find the kinds of jobs they're looking for.

❼ 学生たちと連絡をとっておく

Narrator: The government is **keen** to attract more foreigners to Japan to study **with a view to** tackling the labor shortage. The need to match these students to employers across the country will become **crucial**, putting people such as Lim in even bigger demand. Kentaro Saeki, NHK World.

Review the Key Expressions

各問、選択肢から適切な単語を選び、英文を完成させましょう。なお、余分な単語が 1 語ずつあります。

1. この奨学金に申し込むには、申込用紙に記入しなければいけません。

To (　　　　　) (　　　　　) this scholarship, you (　　　　　) to (　　　　　) (　　　　　) an (　　　　　) form.

out　application　have　take　fill　for　apply

2. 運よく、私は自分の化学の知識［背景］を利用することができた。

(　　　　　), I (　　　　　) (　　　　　) to (　　　　　) (　　　　　) my background in (　　　　　).

draw　able　can　chemistry　on　was　fortunately

3. その男性はデパートの顧客クレームの担当である。

The man is (　　　　　) (　　　　　) of (　　　　　) (　　　　　) customer (　　　　　) at the (　　　　　) store.

with　charge　department　order　dealing　complaints　in

4. 米国は不法移民［移住］を減らすため［〜をもくろんで］、メキシコの国境に外国人を引き留めている。

The U.S. is (　　　　　) foreigners at the Mexican border (　　　　　) a (　　　　　) (　　　　　) reducing (　　　　　) (　　　　　).

immigration　with　detaining　to　view　objection　illegal

● Discussion Questions

1. What kind of jobs are you interested in doing in the future?

2. Would your parents or guardian approve of your working abroad? Why or why not?

UNIT 7

Fighting Food Waste

食品のむだをなくせ！
── スマホ利用のビジネス

パーティーやレストランで残った料理がどれだけの量か、どう処分されるかなどについて一度は考えたことがあると思う。昨今、食料廃棄問題に対して人々の意識が少しずつ変わり、むだに破棄せずに別の用途に活用する動きがある。ネット利用や業界どうしの協力で何ができるのか、今の日本の食料事情に焦点を当てる。

● Words & Phrases

CD 14

□ **edible**　食べられる
□ to **turn the tables**　形勢を逆転する
□ **leftover**　残り物の
□ to **drop by**　ちょっと立ち寄る
□ to **overestimate**　～を過大に見積もる
He seems to have *overestimated* his own abilities.
彼は自分の力量を過信していたようだ。
□ **expiration date**　賞味期限（日）
□ **commission**　手数料、歩合い
□ to **discard**　～を捨てる
At festivals, people *discard* a lot of paper plates and cups.
お祭りでは、みんなが多くの紙皿や紙コップを捨てる。
□ **stalk**　茎
□ **shipment**　発送、出荷

Before You Watch

以下は、野菜に関する語彙です。1 ～ 10 の空所に当てはまる英語を下のアルファベット表から見つけ、線で囲みましょう。囲み方は縦、横、斜めのいずれも可能です。

例：レタス　(lettuce)

・アスパラガス	(	[1])	・もやし	bean sprouts	
・なす	(	[2])	・かぼちゃ	(	[6])
・ブロッコリー	broccoli		・きのこ	(	[7])
・きゅうり	(	[3])	・ごぼう	burdock root	
・生姜	(	[4])	・ミニトマト	(	[8]) tomato
・ピーマン	(	[5]) pepper	・ホウレンソウ	(	[9])
・キャベツ	cabbage		・海藻	(	[10])

	1	2	3	4	5	6	7	8	9	10	11	12	13	14	15	16
a	L	A	S	P	E	A	S	C	S	E	A	W	E	E	D	P
b	E	G	G	P	L	A	N	T	H	P	U	M	I	N	T	U
c	T	S	P	I	N	A	C	H	U	E	R	R	K	T	G	M
d	T	A	H	U	N	C	M	U	S	H	R	O	O	M	R	P
e	U	R	P	J	S	G	W	E	E	D	E	R	U	A	E	K
f	C	U	C	U	M	B	E	R	A	S	P	A	Y	X	E	I
g	E	A	T	A	S	P	A	R	A	G	U	S	E	T	N	N

Watch the News　First Viewing

ニュースを見て、内容と合っているものはＴ、違っているものはＦを選びましょう。

1. People in Japan discard about a million tons of edible food every year. [T / F]

2. Approximately 1,000 restaurants are using the new online food rescue service. [T / F]

3. A group of people in Saga Prefecture use the lower part of asparagus stalks to make sweets. [T / F]

Understand the News　Second Viewing

1 ニュースをもう一度見て、各問の空所に入る適切な選択肢を a ～ c から選びましょう。

1. At this Thai restaurant, they take pictures of their dishes to ____.

a. use as displays in the window at the entrance
b. upload for selling food online
c. advertise their business in local magazines

2. The Thai food introduced on the Internet ____.

a. costs about half the original price or less
b. can only be paid for by using cash, not credit cards
c. is sold in bigger portions than regular orders

3. Project manager Satoshi Inada says that one of their goals is to ____.

a. promote the food-saving program in other parts of Asia
b. greatly reduce the prices of rescued food
c. have a local network cut food waste

2 以下の各情報を、ニュースに出てきた順序に並べましょう。

1. The farmer is impressed by the taste of the asparagus cookies.
2. Inada's organization helps the bakery produce sweets.
3. Customers use an app to rescue the leftover food.
4. Customers visit the restaurant to pick up the food that they ordered.

□ → □ → □ → □

3 CD の音声を聞いて、次ページ News Story の❶～❼の文中にある空所に適切な単語を書き入れましょう。音声は 2 回繰り返されます。　CD 15

● News Story

Anchor: Food waste is a huge problem in Japan. ❶ People here throw away nearly six and a half million tons of perfectly **edible** food a year, about ([1]) ([2]) ([3]) ([4]) ([5]) ([6]) delivered worldwide. Now several organizations are trying to **turn the tables** on this wasteful phenomenon.

❶ 食料支援量の〜倍

Narrator: ❷ This popular Thai restaurant in Tokyo sometimes makes ([1]) ([2]) ([3]) ([4]) ([5]) ([6]).

❷ 店が販売できる以上の（量の）料理

***Tomoya Takahashi* (*General Manager, Gapao Shokudo*):** That happens once or twice a week. We usually have to throw it away.

Narrator: So the owner decided to use a new service. First, pictures are taken of the **leftover** dishes. Then, a price is added and the reason they haven't sold. ❸ With the click of an app, customers can rescue the food and ([1]) ([2]) ([3]) ([4]) ([5]) ([6]) ([7]), then **drop by** and pick it up.

❸ 料理代金をクレジットカードで支払う

It costs about half the normal price when purchased through the app. More than 100 restaurants are participating. Some have **overestimated** the number of customers or used ingredients that are approaching their **expiration dates**. Some dishes go for less than a dollar. The firm that operates the app takes a 35 percent **commission**. Officials there say it's a big hit.

***Kazuma Kawagoe* (*CEO,CoCooking*):** ❹ I think this new business idea ([1]) ([2]) ([3]) ([4]) ([5]) ([6]) in a positive, fun way.

❹ 〜が食料廃棄問題を解決する手助けとなる

Narrator: ❺ Meanwhile, a group in Saga Prefecture ([1]) ([2]) ([3]) ([4]) ([5]) ([6]).

❻ Satoshi Inada heads a project ([1]) ([2]) ([3]) ([4]) ([5]).

His organization is working with this bakery to produce sweets, using farm products that are usually **discarded**. They're now focusing on asparagus. The lower **stalks** are usually cut off before **shipment**, but the team decided to use them as an ingredient in a sweet treat.

Koutaro Ando (Asparagus farmer): This part is very delicious. The parts that just emerged from the ground are sweet and taste good.

Narrator: They developed a recipe for a special kind of cookie.

Ando: (*He tastes a freshly baked cookie.*) Amazing! I'm impressed. What would have ended up as waste has turned into such delicious cookies. It's like a dream.

Narrator: Inada is promoting the program across the prefecture.

Masamine Seki (Cafe owner): It would benefit our business if we can cooperate.

Satoshi Inada (Producer, Suten By Project): Our goal is not merely to develop products but also to create a regional network to cut down on food waste. ❼ I want ([1]) ([2]) ([3]) ([4]) ([5]) ([6]).

Narrator: Promoters of this idea are hoping that their efforts will lower the amount of food that's thrown away and food prices as well.

❺ ～が農産廃棄物を減らすために頑張って［働いて］いる

❻ 農家と事業を結びつける

❼ 日本中に私たちのことばを伝える

Review the Key Expressions

各問、選択肢から適切な単語を選び、英文を完成させましょう。なお、余分な単語が 1 語ずつあります。

1. 勉強に集中したければ、携帯電話をオンにして机につくのはいい考えではない。

If you want to ( ) ( ) studying, it's not a good idea to ( ) at your ( ) with your ( ) ( ).

cellphone desk on sit in on focus

2. 体に悪いものばかり食べていると、結局体調が悪くなってしまうよ。

If you ( ) ( ) only ( ) food, you will ( ) ( ) being ( ).

sick keep end eating use up junk

3. 開発業者は多くの古い学校を地域センターに変えた。

A ( ) has ( ) many ( ) schools ( ) ( ) centers.

into old turned community worked developer

4. 減量のため、高カロリーの食物はおさえる［～を減らす］必要があります。

To ( ) ( ), you ( ) to ( ) ( ) on ( ) calorie food.

should need high lose cut weight down

● Discussion Questions

1. Would you use this online service where restaurants offer food at bargain prices? Why?

2. When do you feel you are wasting money? Why do you feel that way? If not, why not?

UNIT 8 Insulator Promises Energy Savings

透明断熱材
―― 期待される省エネ

エアロゲルという固形発泡体は、極めて軽く断熱効果が高い物質とされる。この物質はコストの関係上、生産量に限界があったが、今回京都大学の研究者チームにより安価で製造することが可能になった。将来的に色々な製品に応用される可能性があり、世界的規模でエネルギー節約に貢献することが期待されている。

● Words & Phrases

CD 16

- ☐ **insulator**　断熱材；絶縁体
- ☐ **start-up**　新設企業
- ☐ **innovative**　革新的な
- ☐ **transparent**　透明な
- ☐ **take**　試み、試作　　☐ **aerogel**　エアロゲル
- ☐ to **cue**　～にきっかけを与える、合図を出す
- ☐ **breakthrough**　飛躍的進歩　　☐ **Associate Professor**　准教授
- ☐ **explainer**　説明（するもの）　　☐ **droplet**　水滴
- ☐ **resilient**　弾力のある　　☐ **resin**　樹脂
- ☐ **vital**　決定的な、肝要な
  Enough sleep and proper nutrition are *vital* for good health.
  十分な睡眠と適切な栄養は健康にとても重要である。
- ☐ **sustainable**　持続可能な
  We have to work toward an environmentally *sustainable* society.
  私たちは環境的に持続可能な社会に向けて努力すべきだ。
- ☐ to **embrace**　～を受け入れる

Before You Watch

以下は、省エネや環境に関する記述です。下の枠内から適切な単語を選び、空所に入れましょう。

1. 省エネ運動が世界中で盛んである。
A campaign for ( ) energy is in full swing all over the world.

2. 私たちは乗用車やトラックのための、環境に優しい燃料を求めている。
We are seeking an environmentally-( ) fuel for cars and trucks.

3. すべての工場が再生可能資源を利用すべきだ。
All factories should use ( ) energy.

4. オゾン層は有害な放射線から地球を守る助けになっている。
The ozone ( ) helps to protect the earth from harmful ( ).

5. この便座暖房は消費電力を削減するように設計されている。
This toilet seat warmer is designed to reduce electrical power ( ).

6. 中国の人々は交通渋滞による大気汚染を心配している。
Chinese people are concerned about the air ( ) caused by heavy traffic.

7. 核燃料がとても危険なことは、みんな知っている。
Everybody is well aware that ( ) fuel is extremely dangerous.

8. 温室効果ガスが、地球温暖化を引き起こしている。
Greenhouse gasses are causing global ( ).

9. その古い工場は、かつて大量の産業廃棄物を排出していた。
The old factory used to produce a lot of ( ) waste.

10. このトイレットペーパーは再生紙でできている。
This toilet paper is made of ( ) paper.

consumption	friendly	industrial	layer	nuclear	pollution
radiation	recycled	renewable	saving	warming	

Watch the News

First Viewing

ニュースを見て、内容と合っているものはT、違っているものはFを選びましょう。

1. A group of researchers at a university invented aerogel this year. [T / F]

2. A venture firm is able to make aerogel now. [T / F]

3. Very light coolers can be made using an aerogel mixture. [T / F]

Understand the News　Second Viewing

1 ニュースをもう一度見て、各問の空所に入る適切な選択肢をａ～ｃから選びましょう。

1. In the experiment, where aerogel was heated, ____.

a. its temperature dropped quickly
b. its color hardly changed at all
c. the material stopped melting

2. Nakanishi says his method of manufacturing aerogel ____.

a. creates more water
b. is less complicated
c. costs a lot less

3. Aerogel can be used ____.

a. in the form of a powder
b. to make thicker winter coats
c. for car mirrors

2 ニュースに関して、空所に入る適切な数字を下の枠内から選びましょう。なお、余分な選択肢もあります。

1. The present aerogel is more than (　　　　　) percent air.
2. Over (　　　　　) percent of the cost of electricity can be saved if aerogel windows are used.
3. Aerogel has existed since the (　　　　　)s.
4. It used to cost (　　　　　) yen to make only 10 cm^2 of aerogel.

30	60	80	90	99	1930	1950	1980	10,000	15,000	100,000

3 CD の音声を聞いて、次ページ News Story の❶～❼の文中にある空所に適切な単語を書き入れましょう。音声は２回繰り返されます。　CD 17

● News Story

Anchor: ❶ A Japanese **start-up** is working on an **innovative** material that it says could change the way ([1]) ([2]) ([3]) ([4]) ([5]) ([6]). NHK World went to find out more.

❶ 私たちが暖かくしていたり、涼しくしていたり

Narrator: It looks like glass, but this **transparent** object is actually a new **take** on a material known as **aerogel**. A team at Kyoto University developed the superlight insulating material which is more than 90 percent air.

Take a look. On the left is ordinary glass, on the right, aerogel. A heater placed underneath warms the two materials at the same rate. Thermal imaging shows that the glass immediately turns yellow as it loses heat. The aerogel barely changes.

Masahiro Yamaji set up a venture firm to mass-produce the new material.

Masahiro Yamaji (CEO, Tiem Factory): ❷ On a hot day, even with air-conditioning, almost half the ([1]) ([2]) ([3]) ([4]) ([5]) ([6]). Aerogel windows can help save over 60 percent on [the]*1 electricity bills.

❷ 窓から［を通して］冷風が逃げる

Narrator: Aerogel has been around since the 1930s. ❸ But in the past, ([1]) ([2]) ([3]) ([4]) ([5]), so mass production was impossible.

❸ 作るのに高い費用がかかった

Kazuki Nakanishi (Associate Professor, Kyoto Univ.):*2 The equipment would have cost us one billion yen.

Narrator: **Cue** a **breakthrough** by Kazuki Nakanishi, **Associate Professor** at Kyoto University. But first, an **explainer**. Aerogel is created when water **droplets** in a gel drain away, leaving air in their place. The challenge is to get the gel to bind without using expensive equipment. Professor Nakanishi discovered that a **resilient** form of silicon holds together even when the water is drained at normal temperature and pressure.

Nakanishi: When we use the traditional method with expensive equipment to make aerogel, it costs 10,000 yen to create one piece measuring only ten centimeters square. But with our manufacturing method, we can make something that size for just a few hundred yen.

Narrator: Yamaji says that even with this new method, it's too difficult to create a piece of aerogel big enough for a window, but that could soon change.

Aerogel can be ground into powder for a whole range of other applications. It can be mixed into fiber to produce thin, lightweight winter clothes that protect against the chill. ❹ Or ([1]) ([2]) ([3]) ([4]) ([5]) **resin** in an ultra-light cooler. ❺ It can also be used in ([1]) ([2]) ([3]) ([4]) ([5]) ([6]). The potential is enormous.

❹ それは～と組み合わせられ得る

❺ 車体や車窓

Yamaji: Right now there is no high performance thermal insulator that can match this. Energy conservation is going to be **vital** if we want to maintain a **sustainable** society. ❻ So ([1]) ([2]) ([3]) ([4]) ([5]) ([6]) ([7]) other than to **embrace** this kind of thing.

❻ 選択の余地があるとは思えない

Narrator: ❼ Innovation, such as aerogel, ([1]) ([2]) ([3]) ([4]) ([5]) ([6]). And that will come as good news for anyone who's opened an electricity bill after a long summer.

❼ 世界中に大きな節約を約束する

Notes

＊[1] the が必要　＊[2] 所属はニュース放送時点（2018 年）のもの

Review the Key Expressions

各問、選択肢から適切な単語を選び、英文を完成させましょう。なお、余分な単語が１語ずつあります。

1. 従業員の運動プログラムに取り組むため、（身体）フィットネスの専門家が導員された。

An (　　　　　) on (　　　　　) fitness (　　　　　) been (　　　　　) in to (______) (______) an exercise program for company workers.

on　physical　expert　brought　put　work　has

2. 警察は、中年の男がなぜ 19 人をナイフで襲ったか解明しようとしている。

The (　　　　　) are (　　　　　) to (______) (______) why a middle-aged man (　　　　　) 19 people (　　　　　) knives.

attacked　police　find　trying　checked　with　out

3. 会場周辺の地図をこのメールに添付しました。どうぞご覧になってください。

I have (　　　　　) a map of the (　　　　　) area (　　　　　) this email. Please (______) (______) (______) at it.

attached　look　take　at　to　a　meeting

4. 事故後は救急車を呼ぼうとすること以外に、何をやればいいのか思い浮かばなかった。

I was not (　　　　　) (　　　　　) doing (　　　　　) after the accident, (______) (______) (　　　　　) to get an ambulance.

other　of　anything　trying　than　nothing　aware

● Discussion Questions

1. What do you do to stay comfortable during hot summers and cold winters?

2. If you started a venture firm someday, what kind of business would it probably be? Why?

UNIT 9 The Fight of Their Life

プロレスで元気を！

北海道の根室に社会人プロレスの団体がある。笑いを誘う演出でパフォーマンスを行い、地域発展のために貢献している。今回、遠距離にある道内の小学校から依頼を受けた。レスラーたちは生徒たちに楽しんでもらい、彼らの前途を祝うために全力で興行を行った。主催者は、よい思い出になってくれたらと温かい気持ちを寄せる。

● Words & Phrases

CD 18

- ☐ **troop**　団体、一団
- ☐ **passionate**　情熱的な、熱い
- ☐ to **put on a show**　興行を行う
- ☐ to **close its doors**　閉業［閉鎖、閉校］する
  Last month the old shop *closed its doors* after 70 years in the shoe-making business.
  先月その古いお店は、靴作り 70 年（の歴史）に幕をおろした。
- ☐ **bout**　〈レスリングやボクシングなどの〉一試合、一勝負
- ☐ **out of harm's way**　安全な所に
- ☐ to **take on**　（特に、大きい相手や強い相手）と戦う、取り組む
- ☐ **intimidating**　威圧的な
- ☐ **headbutting**　〈プロレス技の〉頭突き
- ☐ to **gasp**　息をのむ
  I *gasped* in surprise when I heard the news about the traffic accident.
  その交通事故のニュースを聞いたとき、驚きのあまり息をのんだ。
- ☐ to **overwhelm**　～を圧倒する
- ☐ to **turn the tables**　形勢を逆転する
- ☐ **adversary**　対戦相手

Before You Watch

以下は、スポーツに関する語彙です。1～12の空所に当てはまる英語を下のアルファベット表から見つけ、線で囲みましょう。囲み方は縦、横、斜めのいずれも可能です。

例：ボクシングリング　　boxing (ring)

・オリンピック	(1)	・レスリング	(7)
・パラリンピック	Paralympics	・卓球	(8) tennis
・陸上競技	track and (2)	・対戦相手	(9)
・体操競技	(3)	・競争	competition
・格闘技／武道	(4) arts	・勝者	(10)
・サッカー	(5) / football	・敗者	(11)
・バレーボール	volleyball	・運動選手	(12)
・乗馬	horseback (6)	・観客	spectator

	1	2	3	4	5	6	7	8	9	10	11	12	13	14	15	16
a	R	M	G	Y	M	N	A	S	T	I	C	S	W	E	D	R
b	I	A	T	H	L	E	T	E	O	A	U	M	I	L	R	I
c	N	R	T	R	A	C	K	E	U	C	B	R	N	O	A	D
d	G	T	H	U	M	A	N	I	S	H	C	L	N	S	W	I
e	F	I	E	L	D	U	M	P	I	R	E	E	E	E	E	N
f	C	A	W	R	E	S	T	L	I	N	G	M	R	R	R	G
g	O	L	Y	M	P	I	C	S	O	P	P	O	N	E	N	T

Watch the News　　First Viewing

ニュースを見て、内容と合っているものはT、違っているものはFを選びましょう。

1. The wrestlers in this news report are all nonprofessionals. [T / F]

2. This elementary school has opened recently. [T / F]

3. The principal of the school won the fight against Andre. [T / F]

Understand the News　Second Viewing

1 ニュースをもう一度見て、各問の空所に入る適切な選択肢を a 〜 c から選びましょう。

1. These wrestlers practice ____.
  a. after they finish their daily work
  b. every Saturday and Sunday
  c. three days a week

2. Miyamoto, one of the founders, ____.
  a. gave every student a ring name for the day
  b. taught some wrestling moves in the ring
  c. invited all the students to Nemuro City

3. The principal ____.
  a. did better than his opponent during the whole match
  b. reversed the situation during the bout and won the match
  c. had wrestling experience from being in a college circle

2 ニュースに関して、空所に入る適切な数字を下の枠内から選びましょう。なお、余分な選択肢もあります。

1. There are (　　　　　) members in this wrestling troop.
2. This elementary school has a (　　　　　)-year history.
3. There are (　　　　　) students in all in this elementary school.
4. Andre the Giant Panda is (　　　　　) meters tall.

2	3	4	11	15	17	19	70	90	99

3 CD の音声を聞いて、次ページ News Story の❶〜❼の文中にある空所に適切な単語を書き入れましょう。音声は 2 回繰り返されます。　CD 19

● News Story

Narrator: Pro-wrestling fans in the city of Nemuro decided their community needed some fighting spirit. So, they put together a **troop** of their own. ❶ The wrestlers are **passionate**, but ([1]) ([2]) ([3]) ([4]) ([5]) ([6]). All 17 of them are amateurs with day jobs in businesses like banks and dairies. After work, they work out to get ready for the matches.

❶ ユーモアのセンスなしにということではない

Kenji Miyamoto is one of the founders. He owns a toy shop, but in the ring, he is known as The Middle-Aged Tiger. A while back, the group received a request for a performance. ❷ The ([1]) ([2]) ([3]) ([4]) ([5]) ([6]) whose school was to be shut down.

❷ 観客は小学生の子どもたちである

Miyamoto: We thought the children must be quite upset, so we wanted to **put on a show** that would give them some encouragement.

Narrator: The town of Shihoro is about 250 kilometers from Nemuro. Nishikamiotofuke Elementary School was to **close its doors** after 99 years, but not before a ring was built.

The students, all 11 of them, were invited to sit in the front row. From there, Miyamoto escorted them inside the ropes to try out some moves.

Miyamoto: Fall! Fall! One, two, three...!

Narrator: When the real **bouts** began though, the kids were **out of harm's way**. They wouldn't want to have to **take on** *Andre the Giant Panda**.

Students: (*They cheer.*) Go!

Narrator: Standing three meters tall, Andre was an **intimidating** presence. He knocked out his opponent with **headbutting**, his favorite move.

Students: (*They cheer.*) Panda! Panda!

Narrator: ❸ The ([1]) ([2]) ([3]) ([4]) ([5]) ([6]), the principal. The students **gasped** in excitement.

❸ 次のイベントはゲストレスラーの出番だった

Hiroaki Kawakami (Principal, Nishikamiotofuke Elementary School): The 24th principal of Nishikamiotofuke Elementary School, West Highland Kawakami!

Narrator: The principal tackled his opponent but was soon **overwhelmed** and found himself cornered. ❹ The ([1]) ([2]) ([3]) ([4]) ([5]).

❹ 生徒たちは必死に彼を応援し続けた

Students: (*They cheer.*) Principal! Principal!

Narrator: It worked. He **turned the tables** on his **adversary**.

Referee: Fall! Fall! One, two, three...!

Narrator: Victory for the principal.

Students: (*They cheer.*) Principal! Principal!

Girl student: ❺ I'm sad our school is closing, but ([1]) ([2]) ([3]) ([4]) ([5]) ([6]) today.

❺ 私は、みんなで見たことを絶対忘れません

Miyamoto: ❻ I hope ([1]) ([2]) ([3]) ([4]) ([5]) from time to time in the future and are cheered up by it. That would make me very happy.

❻ 子どもたちが今日の興行を思い出す

Narrator: ❼ Life is a fight to the finish, and these kids ([1]) ([2]) ([3]) ([4]) ([5]) ([6]).

❼ ～はまだ、ラウンドの前半［早い回］にいる

Note

＊Andre the Giant（アンドレ・ザ・ジャイアント、1946-93）はフランスのプロレスラーで、身長 2.23m、体重 236kg であった。以前はモンスター・ロシモフと呼ばれていた

Review the Key Expressions

各問、選択肢から適切な単語を選び、英文を完成させましょう。なお、余分な単語が 1 語ずつあります。

1. 減量のため彼は週３回、体育施設で運動すると決めた。

To ( ) ( ), he decided to ( )
( ) at the gym three ( ) a ( ).

week　out　lose　weight　times　train　work

2. この地域で最大の工場が閉鎖すれば、多くの人たちが経済的に困難になるでしょう。

If the biggest ( ) in this area ( ) its ( ),
many people ( ) be ( ) ( ) financially.

trouble　factory　closest　will　closes　in　doors

3. その力士は、人気のある相手とあまり対戦したくなかった。

The sumo ( ) was ( ) to ( )
( ) an ( ) who was so ( ).

on　reluctant　battle　wrestler　opponent　take　popular

4. 真由美が病床についているときに、彼女の親戚がときどき（見舞いに）訪れた。

Mayumi's relatives ( ) her ( ) ( ) to
( ) when she was ( ) in ( ).

bed　often　visited　time　sick　from　time

● Discussion Questions

1. Do you like pro-wrestling? If so, why? If not, why not?

2. Which did you like best: elementary school, junior high school or senior high school? Why?

UNIT 10 Not-So-Human Resources

人手不足 —— AIで解消!?

日本の高齢化が急速に進むなか、社会制度や組織にひずみが出始めて大きな問題になってきている。労働環境もそのひとつで、労働力不足を補い仕事の効率化を図るために大きな注目を浴びているのが、AI［人工知能］である。果たして、人間に代わる、あるいはそれ以上の仕事や作業ができるのか、最近の動きを追った。

● Words & Phrases

CD 20

- ☐ to **gray**　白髪になる、年をとる
- ☐ **pinch**　危機、ピンチ
- ☐ to **bank on**　《口語》〜をあてにする
  Can you *bank on* this new bus service? Will it be able to handle the Olympic crowds?
  この新しいバスの運行はあてになりますか。オリンピックの観客をうまくさばけますか。
- ☐ to **staff**　人を雇用する
- ☐ to **ring ... up**　〈売り上げなど〉を記録する、お会計をする
- ☐ to **run out of**　〜がなくなる
- ☐ to **streamline**　〜を能率的にする
- ☐ to **get on with**　〜を進める
- ☐ to **dive into**　突然（勢いよく）〜し始める
  After Julie finished Harry Potter Book 1, she *dived into* Book 2.
  ジュリーはハリーポッターの第1巻を読み終えると、第2巻に飛びついた。
- ☐ **spike**　急激な上昇

Before You Watch

以下は頭字語や省略語などの問題です。下の枠内の語彙を使って元の形を完成させましょう。必要に応じて語頭を大文字にしてください。なお、余分な単語もあります。

例：AI　人工知能　(artificial) intelligence

1. GDP　国内総生産　gross (　　　　　) product
2. NATO　北大西洋条約機構　North (　　　　　) Treaty Organization
3. BRICS　ブリックス　Brazil, Russia, (　　　　　), China, South Africa
4. brunch　ブランチ　(　　　　　) + lunch
5. TOEFL® トーフル　Test of English as a (　　　　　) Language
6. c.v.　履歴書　(　　　　　) vitae
7. VIP　要人　very (　　　　　) person
8. laser　レーザー　(　　　　　) amplification by stimulated emission of radiation
9. scuba　スキューバ　self-contained (　　　　　) breathing apparatus
10. ASAP　ただちに　as (　　　　　) as possible

arctic	~~artificial~~	athletic	atlantic	brand	bread	breakfast
calcium	curriculum	custom	delivery	domestic	detail	
familiar	foreign	functional	important	intelligent	interesting	
India	Indonesia	Italy	left	leaking	light	
safe	sensible	soon	underground	underwater	unified	

Watch the News

First Viewing

ニュースを見て、内容と合っているものはT、違っているものはFを選びましょう。

1. Artificial intelligence never makes mistakes. [T / F]
2. They started using a cash register equipped with AI in this bakery. [T / F]
3. In this 24-hour supermarket, clerks check the stock around five times a day. [T / F]

Understand the News　Second Viewing

1 ニュースをもう一度見て、各問の空所に入る適切な選択肢を a～c から選びましょう。

1. In this bakery, ____.
  a. many products look alike to people
  b. they sell more than 30 different items
  c. it is not too difficult to hire elderly workers

2. At the bakery shown in this report, there ____.
  a. are now 30 full-time employees
  b. used to be 15 workers on a full-time basis
  c. were bakers who also worked as cashiers

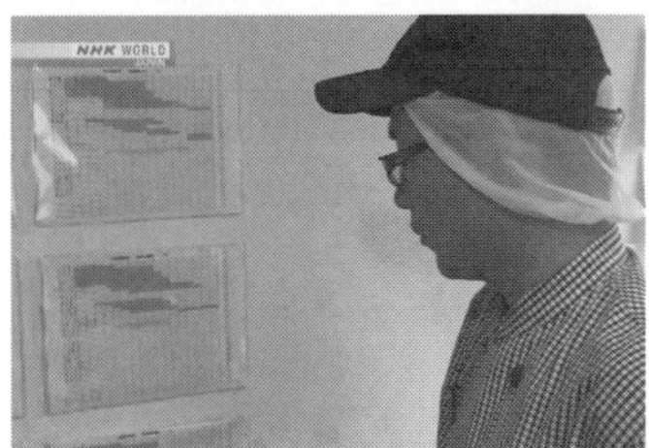

3. AI cameras inside this supermarket collect information about ____.
  a. whether customers need assistance or not
  b. what merchandise shoppers put their hands on
  c. where their customers come from

2 次の各文を読み、ニュースの内容に合っているものを 1 つ選びましょう。

1. The bakery in this report is located in a supermarket chain.
2. In this bakery, the new cash register looks like a humanoid robot.
3. Once more part-timers are hired, the bakery is going to get rid of the AI register.
4. In this supermarket, the AI cameras send graphs to the business manager.
5. Bananas are always popular items at this supermarket.

3 CD の音声を聞いて、次ページ News Story の❶～❼の文中にある空所に適切な単語を書き入れましょう。音声は 2 回繰り返されます。　CD 21

● News Story

Anchor: Japan's **graying** population means labor shortages are a big problem for many kinds of businesses. Retailers are feeling the **pinch** even more than most, but some are finding that AI has the answer.

Narrator: This bakery is **banking on** a new kind of cash register to solve its **staffing** problems. ❶ A ([1]) ([2]) ([3]) ([4]) ([5]) ([6]), and a computer identifies the products and **rings** them **up**.

❶ カメラがパンの画像をとらえる

It's not an easy task. Many bakery items look alike to the human eye. And the computer has to account for the variations in color and shape that come with baking. But the cash register has artificial intelligence and can learn from its mistakes. ❷ So ([1]) ([2]) ([3]) ([4]) ([5]) ([6]).

❷ 常に改善されている

Norichika Inoue ***(Bakery Moisson):*** The more we use it, the more precisely it can *distinguish the breads**.

Narrator: The shop turned to this register because of a serious labor shortage. ❸ For the past few years the manager ([1]) ([2]) ([3]) ([4]) ([5]) ([6]) to fill all the vacancies.

❸ 人を見つけることができなかった

There used to be about 30 workers. Now there is only about half that number. And the shop often **ran out of** products as a result.

Inoue: ❹ The baking staff ([1]) ([2]) ([3]) ([4]) ([5]) ([6]), working the cash register. And as a result, we weren't baking fast enough, and our shelves ended up empty. That was really tough.

❹ ときどき両方の職務を行わなければならなかった

Narrator: The new cash register with its digital brain has **streamlined** the payment process and freed up the staff to **get on with** the baking.

A national 24-hour supermarket chain is **diving into** AI too. Its latest stores are equipped with 700 AI cameras. ❺ They are able to detect ([1]) ([2]) ([3]) ([4]) ([5]) ([6]) or even monitor which products customers are touching. The computer compiles the data and sends graphs to the manager.

❺ いつ棚に品物が不足するか

In this instance, there was a sudden **spike** in the sales of bananas.

Manager: ❻ ([1]) ([2]) ([3]) ([4]), ([5]).

❻ もっとバナナを出して［補充して］ください

Narrator: In the old days staff would walk around the store five times a day to check the stock, and the shelves were often empty.

Shop clerk: It's very easy now. We don't have to keep walking round and round.

Narrator: The store manager says the technology doesn't just save on staffing needs. ❼ It makes life easier ([1]) ([2]) ([3]) ([4]) ([5]) ([6]). And that makes it easier to hire people.

❼ そこで働く人たちにとって

Note

＊ ここは distinguish among the breads だとわかりやすい

Review the Key Expressions

各問、選択肢から適切な単語を選び、英文を完成させましょう。なお、余分な単語が 1 語ずつあります。

1. 学問は、学べば学ぶほど、もっと学ぶことがあることがわかる。

The ( ) we learn, the ( ) we ( ) there ( ) to ( ) ( ).

find more here be more is learned

2. 時間がなくなりました。来週［今日から一週間後に］話し合いを再開しましょう。

We ( ) just ( ) ( ) of time. Let's ( ) our ( ) a ( ) from today.

week run have discussion resume almost out

3. キャンプをしている間に、大雨が降ってきた。結果として、ハイキングの計画はむだになった。

It started ( ) ( ) we were camping. As a ( ), our plans to take a ( ) have gone ( ) the ( ).

hike drain pouring rule result while down

4. 10 分休んでから、運転技術の次のステップ、坂道駐車に進みましょう。

Let's ( ) a ten-minute ( ) and then ( ) ( ) with the next step in learning to ( ), ( ) on a hill.

break on drive take parking get down

● Discussion Questions

1. Do you think people will lose jobs because of AI? If so, in what fields? If not, why not?

2. There is a match-making service which uses AI to match singles. Would you use such a service? Why?

UNIT 11

Adapting to a Tourist Influx

「宿坊」人気
―― 海外からの訪問客

瞑想で自分を見つめ、黙々と写経をし、丹精込めて用意された精進料理をいただく。いま外国人観光客の間で宿坊に泊まる旅が人気を博している。過去に色々な誤解やトラブルがあったが、寺院側も積極的に英語で対応し、仏教についての説明もするようになった。日本への訪問客が増えるなか、最近の宿坊事情をレポートする。

● Words & Phrases

CD 22

- ☐ **influx**　到来、殺到
- ☐ **scenery**　景色、景観
- ☐ **spike**　急激な上昇
- ☐ **cheers**　乾杯

  To our continuing friendship and teamwork. *Cheers*!

  私たちの継続する友情とチームワークに。乾杯！
- ☐ to **inhale**　息を吸い込む
- ☐ **meditation**　瞑想
- ☐ **teaching**　教え
- ☐ **growing pains**　《事業など》初期の困難、産みの苦しみ

  The company is experiencing *growing pains* now.

  その会社は今、苦労しながら成長している。
- ☐ **curfew**　門限
- ☐ to **restrict**　～を制限する

Before You Watch

以下は、日本の宗教に関する記述です。下の枠内から適切な単語を選び、空所に入れましょう。

1. 神道は古代からの伝統的な日本の宗教だ。
Shintoism is the ancient ( ) religion of Japan.

2. 仏教は6世紀に日本に伝来した。
Buddhism was ( ) to Japan in the 6th ( ).

3. 多くの日本人は、神道と仏教の両方の宗教（行事）を実践している。
Many Japanese people ( ) both Shintoism and Buddhism.

4. 自然の力を含め、神道には多くの神がいる。
There are many ( ) in Shintoism, including ( ) spirits.

5. 神道には創始者もいなければ、正規の経典もない。
Shintoism has no ( ) and no official scripture.

6. 日本人は結婚時などお祝いごとがあるときは神社に行く。
Japanese people visit shrines to ( ) happy life events, such as getting married.

7. 仏教は、どのようにして煩悩を取り除くか、精神的な悟りを得るかを教え諭す。
Buddhism teaches people how to eliminate ( ) temptations and to attain spiritual ( ).

8. 葬儀や法要はお寺で営まれる。
Funerals and ( ) services are ( ) at Buddhist temples.

awakening	century	earthly	founder	gods	held
introduced	mark	memorial	nature	practice	traditional

Watch the News

First Viewing

ニュースを見て、内容と合っているものはT、違っているものはFを選びましょう。

1. At these Buddhist ceremonies, the participants are mostly Japanese tourists. [T / F]
2. In this basic meditation session, there are explanations in English. [T / F]
3. The chief priest of Fumonin Temple has never studied English before. [T / F]

Understand the News　Second Viewing

1 ニュースをもう一度見て、各問の空所に入る適切な選択肢をａ～ｃから選びましょう。

1. According to this news, nighttime activities include ____.

a. a visit to a cemetery
b. hand-copying teachings from Sanskrit literature
c. a meditation session

2. Organizer Nobuhiro Tamura suggests that ____.

a. he wants to help tourists take good pictures
b. tourists usually are unaware of Buddhist teachings
c. Japanese people should talk more about their religions

3. Honjun Kondo, Chief Priest of Fumonin says ____.

a. their temple should limit the number of foreign tourists
b. curfews are not necessary for their temple anymore
c. they should accept foreign visitors at their lodgings

2 以下の各情報を、ニュースに出てきた順序に並べましょう。

1. A monk explains the importance of spending time on meditation.
2. There are a lot of foreign tourists who visit the Koyasan region to experience something spiritual.
3. The temple restricted visits by foreigners for many years.
4. Foreign visitors have caused some trouble such as wearing shoes inside of the temple buildings.

3 CD の音声を聞いて、次ページ News Story の❶～❼の文中にある空所に適切な単語を書き入れましょう。音声は 2 回繰り返されます。　CD 23

● News Story

Narrator: This is a Shingon Buddhist ceremony. The participants are mostly foreign tourists. They come to the Koyasan region for the **scenery**, the history and the sample of something spiritual.

❶ ([1]) ([2]) ([3]) ([4]) ([5]). In recent years a **spike** in foreign tourists *have**1 replaced a drop in domestic visitors. ❷ Today's Japanese ([1]) ([2]) ([3]) ([4]) ([5]) ([6]) as previous generations.

❶ 多くの人が寺院に宿泊する

❷ (〜と) 同じような関心は示さない

Foreign guests: (*Before they eat*) **Cheers**!

Narrator: At this temple 70 percent of guests are now from overseas.

Daigen Kondo ***(Chief priest, Ekoin):*** You learn so much just by staying overnight. It gives you a feeling of what Koyasan Shingon Buddhism is all about.

Monk: **Inhale** and exhale....

Narrator: The monks saw the trend and many have adapted. This basic **meditation** session comes with English explanations.

Monk: In modern life we are too busy. ❸ You ([1]) ([2]), ([3]) ([4]) ([5]) ([6]), go to work. It might be nice to have some minutes to think nothing.

❸ 目が覚めて、携帯をチェックして

Narrator: And there are nighttime activities, including a tour of one of the country's oldest cemeteries.

Monk: The moon is quite important in our **teaching**.

Narrator: ❹ This monk says he started offering the tours because he noticed many visitors came ([1]) ([2]) ([3]) ([4]) ([5]) ([6]). He says he wants to help them understand the spiritual side of things.

❹ ただ写真を何枚か撮るためだけに

***Nobuhiro Tamura* (Organizer):** There are Buddhist, Buddhist teachings everywhere in this town, okay? But they miss, miss all of them, okay? ❺ I ([1]) ([2]) ([3]) ([4]) ([5]) ([6]).

❺ この状況はまったく情けなかった

(At Fumonin Temple)

Narrator: Some of the other temples that [were forced]*[2] to change, say they too see the benefit of the new tourism wave.

***Honjun Kondo* (Chief Priest):** (*He practices English.*) ❻ ([1]) ([2]) ([3]) ([4]) ([5]) Fumonin....

❻ このお寺をご紹介いたします

Narrator: The chief priest here is studying English again for the first time in decades. But he says the shift hasn't been without **growing pains**. Foreign visitors caused trouble in the past by wearing shoes inside, a real no-no in Japan. They also ignored **curfew**. So, for many years the temple **restricted** *entrance to them**[3]. ❼ But recently ([1]) ([2]) ([3]) ([4]) ([5]) ([6]) in order to survive.

❼ そのお寺［それ］は海外からの旅行者［彼ら］を再び迎え入れることにした

Honjun Kondo: It's one way to pass on the history and culture of Koyasan to future generations. It's high time we started accepting foreign people at our lodgings.

Monk: We thank you for coming here.

Narrator: This place that's been known for its harmony, is now trying to achieve a new balance. Takaya Kawasaki, NHK World, Koyasan, Wakayama.

Notes

*[1] 文法的には単数形 has

*[2] 発音が不明瞭だが that were forced のような意味の節がくるのが妥当

*[3] *entrance to them* は their entrance のほうがふつうの言い方

Review the Key Expressions

各問、選択肢から適切な単語を選び、英文を完成させましょう。なお、余分な単語が 1 語ずつあります。

1. メニューにあるどのサンドウィッチも、S サイズのフライドポテトと冷たいドリンクがついてきます。

( ) sandwich on the menu ( ) ( ) a small ( ) of ( ) ( ) and a cold drink.

comes each fries with either French serving

2. 先週、幼稚園以来初めて両親と一緒にディズニーランドへ行った。

Last week my ( ) and I went to the Disneyland ( ) the ( ) time ( ) I was ( ) ( ).

in parents for kindergarten since during first

3. 旅行に参加したいならここに名前を書いて、リストを次の人にまわしてください。

If you want to ( ) ( ) for the ( ), write your name ( ), and then ( ) the list ( ) to the next person.

on sign here give up pass trip

4. そろそろ自分の将来のことを考えたらどうですか［～するのにいい時期だ］。

It's ( ) ( ) you ( ) ( ) about ( ) ( ).

future period thinking time started your high

● Discussion Questions

1. Would you like to stay at a temple and experience Buddhist services, the hand-copying of sutras and vegetarian cuisine? Why or why not?

2. What's the best way for you to study English: watch movies, read newspapers, write in journals? Why?

UNIT 12 Japan's Creative Classrooms

英語は楽しく学べ！

日本人が英会話が苦手なのはよく指摘されることだが、対策をたてる努力を怠っているわけではない。過去においても英語指導教員［AET］の導入があったが、今度は AI ロボットの活用やイマージョン［英語浸け］プログラムが注目されている。果たしてこれらが英会話学習の追い風となるのか、期待の声も大きい。

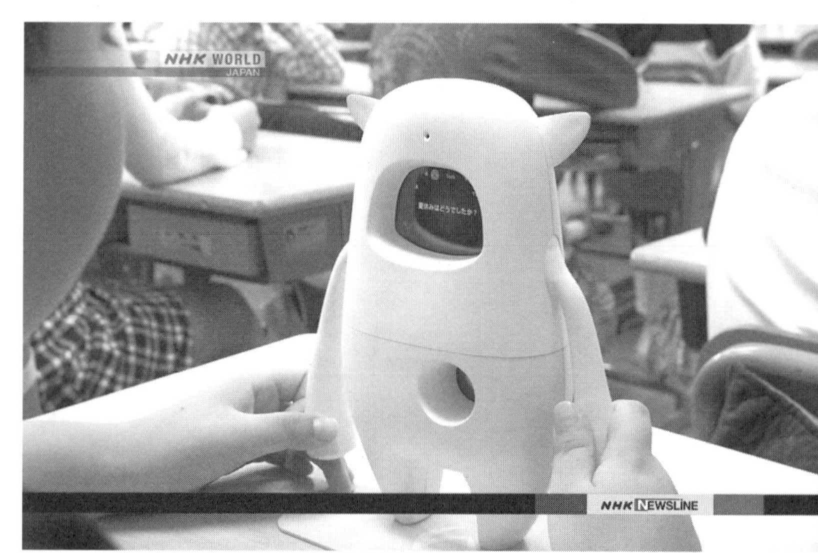

● Words & Phrases

CD 24

- □ to **turn things around**　事態を好転させる、立ち直らせる
- □ **grader**　～年生〈大学生には使用しない〉
  These students are sixth *graders*.　この生徒たちは小学6年生です。
- □ to **accumulate**　～を蓄積する
- □ to **tailor**　～を作る、～を仕立てる
- □ **optimal**　最適の、最善の
  For *optimal* learning, review your notes immediately after class.
  最適な学習のためには、授業後すぐに講義メモを復習しなさい。
- □ **Board of Education**　教育委員会
- □ **immersive**　没入型の、集中型の〈名詞形は immersion〉
- □ **pharmacist**　薬剤師
- □ to **complement**　補完する
  This hat *complements* her dress beautifully.
  この帽子が彼女のドレスを美しく映えさせている。
- □ **workforce**　労働力

Before You Watch

以下は、教師が授業で使う表現です。下の枠内から適切な語彙を選び、空所に入れましょう。

1. どこでもいいので座ってください。それでは、（授業を）始めましょう。
You can sit ( ) you want. Let's get ( ) now.

2. この前は 46 ページの 5 行目までやりました。
Last time we ( ) ( ) on page 46, line 5.

3. （私の説明が）じゅうぶんわかりましたか。
Did I express ( ) clearly enough?

4. みなさんには（授業のペースが）ちょっと早すぎますか。
Am I ( ) too fast for you?

5. これはみなさんが思うほど難しくありません。
This is ( ) ( ) difficult as you might think.

6. 新しい単語が出てきたら、辞書で調べてください。
When you come ( ) a new word, ( ) it up in your dictionary.

7. 大変よくできました。 Excellent! / Well ( )! / You did a good ( )!

8. もう少し大きな声で言ってください。 Can you ( ) ( ) a little?

9. このプリントをやって提出してください。
Complete this ( ) and ( ) it in.

10. みなさんの（最終）成績は、このテストがすべてではありません。
Your final ( ) won't be ( ) on this one exam.

across	anyplace	as	based	done	going	grade	handout	job
left	look	myself	not	off	speak	started	turn	up

Watch the News

First Viewing

ニュースを見て、内容と合っているものは T、違っているものは F を選びましょう。

1. Last year's TOEIC® results indicated that the English-speaking ability of Japanese was very low. [T / F]

2. According to a principal, AI robots can be a great help in language study. [T / F]

3. The male worker who was interviewed has a job in a drugstore in real life. [T / F]

Understand the News　Second Viewing

1 ニュースをもう一度見て、各問の空所に入る適切な選択肢をａ～ｃから選びましょう。

1. Tokyo's Board of Education and ____ started an English immersion program.
a. an English teaching company
b. a travel agency
c. a private high school

2. An expert's opinion is that immersive environments can ____ the school's English program.
a. take over
b. spoil
c. supplement

3. The new immersive program has received reservations from about ____ people.
a. 500　**b.** 5,000　**c.** 50,000

2 以下はニュースの概要です。空所に適切な単語を書き入れましょう。語頭の文字(群)は与えてあります。

Japanese people in general are not good at speaking English. An elementary school in Tokyo is getting some help from robots (**eq** 1) with AI. These robots can (**com** 2) in English with students. The principal of the school feels there is excellent (**po** 3) for the use of such robots.

The Tokyo Board of Education started an (**im** 4) learning center with the help of a language school. The students speak only English with (**fo** 5) staff all day long. Their program is very popular, although the facility opened only (**l** 6) month.

3 CDの音声を聞いて、次ページNews Storyの❶～❼の文中にある空所に適切な単語を書き入れましょう。音声は2回繰り返されます。 CD 25

● News Story

Anchor: Japanese education officials have been watching the economy become over...or ever more globalized and worry their students might get left behind. Last year's TOEFL® test results had Japan lowest among Asian countries for speaking ability. ❶ Our next report ([1]) ([2]) ([3]) ([4]) ([5]) the authorities are trying to **turn things around**.

Narrator: Students at a school near Tokyo are getting some high-tech help.

Student: (*He chooses a robot.*) I like this one.

Narrator: The robots are equipped with artificial intelligence and can chat in English with the 5th and 6th **graders**.

Boy student: How was your summer holiday?

AI Robot: ❷ ([1]) ([2]) ([3]) ([4]) ([5]) ([6]).

Girl student: How was it?

AI Robot: It was very fun.

Narrator: The principal sees great potential for AI robots in the classroom.

Mieko Odaka (Principal, Toda Dai-2 elementary school): ❸ The devices could **accumulate** data and build ([1]) ([2]) ([3]) ([4]) ([5]) ([6]). They could then analyze that data to **tailor** the **optimal** program for each student.

Narrator: In Tokyo, the **Board of Education** has teamed up with a private language school to open a new kind of **immersive** learning center. ❹ The idea is to create realistic settings ([1]) ([2]) ([3]) ([4]) ([5]).

❶ 創造的なやり方を紹介する[見る]

❷ 遊園地に行ったよ

❸ その子どもの成績評価

❹ 生徒たちの動機づけをする

Man: Hello, I'm a **pharmacist**.

Woman: I'm the flight *attendant**[1].

Narrator: There's a hotel, a shop and a fast-food restaurant among other settings.

Teacher: I want to eat because I need to leave.

Student: (*He repeats.*) I want to eat because I...

Teacher: (*He urges the student to repeat.*) I need to leave.

Student: (*He repeats.*) I need to leave.

Teacher: (*He urges him to repeat again.*) to leave early.

Student: (*He repeats.*) to [leave]*[2] early.

Teacher: Yes. Good. ❺ ([1]) ([2]) ([3]) ([4]) ([5]) ([6])!

❺ そう、その調子です

Student: ❻ ([1]) ([2]) ([3]) ([4]) ([5]) to speak English, so I'm glad to have one here.

❻ いつもチャンスがあるわけではありません

Narrator: The company's CEO says he thinks the immersive environments can **complement** the lessons students take at school.

***Nobuo Oda* (*President CEO, Tokyo Global Gateway*):** The excitement the students feel when they're able to communicate with foreign staff gives them an enthusiasm to learn English more and to speak more. And that feeds back into the classrooms in their normal schools to create a virtual cycle.

Narrator: ❼ The facility opened last month and ([1]) ([2]) ([3]) ([4]) ([5]) ([6]). It says it's taken bookings from nearly 50,000 people. The education officials know there's a lot to do, but they're hoping ideas like these are small steps *in**[3] the path to a global **workforce**.

❼ すでに大盛況だということがわかった[～を証明した]

Notes

*[1] 不要な –s が語尾で発音されている　*[2] leave の挿入が期待されるところ　*[3] on のほうがよい

Review the Key Expressions

各問、選択肢から適切な単語を選び、英文を完成させましょう。なお、余分な単語が１語ずつあります。

1. その会社は倒産しそうだったが、新しいCEO［最高経営責任者］が事態を好転させた。

The (　　　　　) almost (　　　　　) (　　　　　), but the new CEO (　　　　　) (　　　　　) (　　　　　).

around　went　in　things　turned　company　bankrupt

2. まもなく香港のバスに、最新の安全手段が備えられると聞いた。

I (　　　　　) buses in Hong Kong (　　　　　) soon (　　　　　) (　　　　　) with (　　　　　) (　　　　　) measures.

be　satisfied　safety　heard　will　state-of-the-art　equipped

3. ユニークな小型自動車を生産するために、そのベンチャー企業が自動車製造業者と手を組んだ。

The (　　　　　) firm (　　　　　) (　　　　　) (　　　　　) an (　　　　　) to (　　　　　) unique small cars.

up　automaker　with　produce　venture　came　teamed

4. マイクとめぐみは結婚して何年にもなるが、いまだにお互いに意思疎通することが困難である。

Mike and Megumi (　　　　　) been (　　　　　) for (　　　　　), but they still have a (　　　　　) time (　　　　　) with (　　　　　) other.

hard　married　each　marry　communicating　years　have

● Discussion Questions

1. What are some advantages and disadvantages of English immersion programs?

2. Is it a good idea to study English in kindergarten or elementary school? Why?

UNIT 13

New Spin on Laundromats

コインランドリー最前線

日本のコインランドリーは1960年代の登場以来、利用客に使い勝手のいいサービスが模索されてきた。最近では特に多忙な人たちをターゲットとして、ネット利用の情報サービス、待ち時間の有効活用、他の施設との併設の有無、防犯対策などが集客に大きく影響している。業界の企業努力と顧客の利便性の現在を報告する。

● Words & Phrases

CD 26

□ **laundromat**　〈米、カナダなどの〉コインランドリー〈英国ではlaundretteという〉

□ **humble**　ささやかな、控えめな

I run a *humble* cafe in the neighborhood where I was born and raised.

私は生まれ育った地域にささやかなカフェを経営している。

□ **era**　時代

□ **top-of-the-line**　最高級品の

□ **full-fledged**　本格的な、一人前の

The country has become a *full-fledged* military power.

その国は、正真正銘の軍事大国になった。

□ **premises**　店舗、店内

□ **unit**　（完全な）1つのもの、1個

□ to **stand to**　～を得る立場にある

□ **chore**　（面倒な、つらい）雑用、家事

□ **currency**　通貨

□ **power outlet**　電源

□ **ubiquitous**　どこにでもある、遍在する

Before You Watch

以下は、家庭用の機械・装置類に関する語彙です。下記の枠内から適切な単語を選び、空所に入れましょう。

1. 洗濯機	(	) machine
2. 掃除機	(	) cleaner
3. エアコン	air (	)
4. 除湿機	(	)
5. 換気扇	(	) fan
6. インターホン	(	)
7. 防犯カメラ	(	) camera
8. 蛍光灯	(	) light
9. 炊飯器	(	) cooker
10. オーブントースター	toaster (	)
11. ミキサー	(	)
12. 食品乾燥器	food (	)
13. 浄水器	water (	)
14. 蒸し器	(	)

blender	conditioner	dehumidifier	dehydrator	
fluorescent	intercom	oven	purifier	rice
security	steamer	vacuum	ventilation	washing

Watch the News

First Viewing

ニュースを見て、内容と合っているものはT、違っているものはFを選びましょう。

1. Laundromats are becoming popular again. [T / F]

2. Only coins are accepted by Tosei's laundry machines. [T / F]

3. Laundromat operators want to help users enjoy the time spent washing. [T / F]

Understand the News　Second Viewing

1 ニュースをもう一度見て、各問の空所に入る適切な選択肢をa～cから選びましょう。

1. The Japanese laundromat version 2.0 has a ____.
  a. cafe that half the laundry's customers use
  b. dry cleaning and clothing repair service
  c. fitness club where instructors are available

2. Some new machines provide online information about ____.
  a. neighborhood traffic and weather
  b. the number of washing machines available
  c. local shopping and events

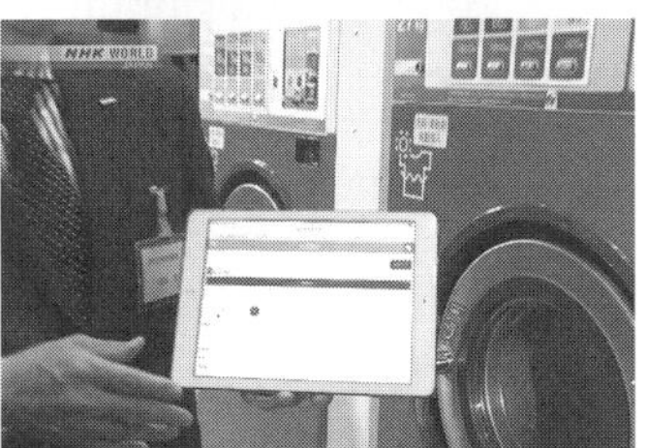

3. Tosei is going to ____.
  a. enlarge the space for customers
  b. start more new laundromats
  c. sell local fruits and vegetables

2 次の各文を読み、ニュースの内容に合っているものを2つ選びましょう。

1. More and more laundromats are providing space for kids.
2. Washing machines are being improved as well as laundromat premises.
3. Some new services are designed for smartphone users.
4. Full-fledged climbing walls are most popular on this laundromat's premises.
5. Laundromats have become as ubiquitous as convenience stores.

3 CDの音声を聞いて、次ページNews Storyの❶～❼の文中にある空所に適切な単語を書き入れましょう。音声は2回繰り返されます。　CD 27

● News Story

Anchor: ❶ In our feature we look at why the **humble laundromat** is making a comeback in an **era** when ([1]) ([2]) ([3]) ([4]) ([5]) ([6]) at home.

❶ ほとんどの人たちが洗濯機を持っている

Narrator: Meet the Japanese laundromat, version 2-point-oh (2.0). It comes with **top-of-the-line** washers, dryers and a cafe. The operator is hoping to make the 30- to 60-minute wait simply more enjoyable. More than 50 percent of customers take advantage of the cafe.

Those who would rather not sit for half an hour have other options, such as this laundromat equipped with a **full-fledged** climbing wall.

But it's not just the **premises** that are changing. The machines are evolving, too. These models are connected to the Internet. They allow users to check online how many **units** are available. So no more time [is]*[1] wasted waiting for an open slot.

Coin laundry operators also **stand to** benefit. ❷ They can track data in real time and, for example, ([1]) ([2]) ([3]) when ([4]) ([5]) ([6]).

❷ お客さんがあまりいない（ときに）特価で提供する

Tsuneki Yoshida (COO, Aqua Japan): ❸ Laundromats have ([1]) ([2]) ([3]) ([4]) ([5]) ([6]) in allowing people to deal with house **chores** more efficiently. ❹ I believe this business ([1]) ([2]) ([3]) ([4]) ([5]).

❸ 重要な役割を演じるようになった

❹ かなりの伸びしろがある

Narrator: With competition increasing, some manufacturers are moving quickly to seize the opportunity. This laundromat run by Tosei caters primarily to the smartphone generation. ❺ ([1]) ([2]) ([3])

❺ 日本中のほとんどのコンビニのように

(4) (5) (6), it accepts payments in digital **currency**. ❻ **Power outlets** let users (1) (2) (3) (4) (5) (6).

❻ 待っている間に自分のデバイスを充電する

Tosei plans to open more laundromats in large cities and market them as *user-friendly environment*[s]*[2].

***Takehiko Takahashi* (Director, Tosei):** We are confident that our machines provide a top quality finish. Once users understand that, I believe laundromats will become as **ubiquitous** as convenience stores.

Narrator: ❼ Doing the laundry (1) (2) (3) (4) (5) (6), but one that has to be done. Laundromat operators are hoping to make the time people spend in their facilities more relaxing or even more productive.

❼ 常に、楽しくない仕事だった

Notes

*[1] 文にするにはここに is が必要

*[2] *a user-friendly environment* と読まれているが、user-friendly environments が適切

Review the Key Expressions

各問、選択肢から適切な単語を選び、英文を完成させましょう。なお、余分な単語が 1 語ずつあります。

1. よい天気を利用して、ビーチに行きましょう。

We should ( ) ( ) ( ) the good ( ) and ( ) ( ) the beach.

of go advantage convenience to weather take

2. 歴史が始まって以来［～を通して］、日本人は台風や地震のような多くの自然災害を経験してきた。

( ) history, Japanese people ( ) ( ) a lot of ( ) disasters ( ) ( ) typhoons and earthquakes.

natural have as throughout such experienced though

3. その会社のオーナーが亡くなったら、彼の子どもたちが何百万ドルも相続する立場にある。

( ) the owner of the company ( ), his children ( ) ( ) inherit ( ) of ( ).

dies millions to dollars after thousands stand

4. このニュースチャンネルは、日本中からの交通情報を即時提供している。

This news channel ( ) traffic information ( ) ( ) ( ) from ( ) ( ) Japan.

off over provides in time all real

● Discussion Questions

1. What is the chore you most dislike: doing the laundry, washing dishes, cleaning, shopping? Why?

2. What is one machine or device that you can't live without? Why?

UNIT 14 Budget Train Gives Rich Rewards

節約観光列車
── おもてなしの工夫

北海道南部の海沿いを走る「ながまれ海峡号」という観光列車での旅が日本一の鉄道旅行に選ばれた。北海道新幹線の開業に伴い、JRが経営を切り離した赤字路線だった。それを第三セクターが引き継ぎ「のんびり、ゆっくり」を売りに、人気の観光列車に変身させた。地元の人々はどのような手段で集客に成功したのだろうか。

● Words & Phrases

CD 28

- ☐ **hat**　仕事、役割、肩書き
- ☐ **gamut**　全範囲、ありとあらゆるもの
- ☐ **semipublic**　第三セクターの、半公共的な
- ☐ to **take over**　～を引き継ぐ
- ☐ **budget projections**　予算見積もり
- ☐ **shortfall**　不足（額）
- ☐ to **lure**　～を引き付ける
- ☐ to **enlist**　〈人〉に協力を求める；〈人の援助など〉を得る
  We need to *enlist* the help of young people to revitalize the town.
  町を活性化させるためには、若い人の助けを求める必要がある。
- ☐ to **draw to a close**　終わりに近づく
  The party *drew to a close* around nine p.m.
  パーティーは午後9時頃終わりに近づいた。
- ☐ **squid fishing boat**　イカ釣り船

Before You Watch

以下は、日本の食（文化）に関する語彙です。下記の枠内から適切な単語を選び、空所に入れましょう。なお、余分な単語もあります。

1.	餡（あん）	sweet ( ) jam
2.	焼き芋	baked ( ) potato
3.	納豆	( ) beans
4.	豆腐	bean ( )
5.	焼き鳥	grilled chicken on a ( )
6.	うどん	( ) noodles
7.	そば	( ) noodles
8.	親子丼	( ) and egg bowl
9.	牛丼	( ) bowl
10.	お好み焼き	meat［あるいは seafood］and vegetable ( )
11.	さしみ	sliced ( ) fish
12.	もち	rice ( )
13.	団子	steamed ball of ( ) flour
14.	だし	soup ( )

bean	beef	buckwheat	cake	chicken	curd	
eggroll	fermented	octopus	pancake	pork	raw	
rice	skewer	stock	sweet	tea	wheat	

Watch the News

First Viewing

ニュースを見て、内容と合っているものはT、違っているものはＦを選びましょう。

1. The Nagamare Kaikyo sightseeing cruiser runs every day. [T / F]

2. The sightseeing train makes four-hour round-trips. [T / F]

3. The railroad company depends on local people to help with the program. [T / F]

Understand the News　　Second Viewing

1 ニュースをもう一度見て、各問の空所に入る適切な選択肢をａ～ｃから選びましょう。

1. Remodeling the Nagamare Kaikyo train cost ____ dollars.
- **a.** 90,000
- **b.** 900,000
- **c.** 90,000,000

2. One problem the railroad company faced was that ____.
- **a.** it was too cold in the winter
- **b.** there wasn't a big fish market representing this area
- **c.** there were no major tourist spots

3. Community residents ____.
- **a.** get together to make *bekomochi*
- **b.** offer to help serve local seafood
- **c.** were invited to ride the ultra-luxury sleeper train

2 以下はニュースの概要です。空所に適切な単語を書き入れましょう。語頭の文字(群)は与えてあります。

The Nagamare Kaikyo Train Line is a local line in the south part of Hokkaido. When they couldn't make enough money, a (**se** [1]) railway company took over the line. To attract more (**pa** [2]), the company started sightseeing tours. They didn't have much money to (**re** [3]) the train, so the company (**en** [4]) the help of local people. A baker made a local rice cake product, and many helped prepare a (**s** [5]) BBQ. Thanks to all the efforts, the line won the (**g** [6]) prize in a Japanese railroad tour contest.

3 CD の音声を聞いて、次ページ News Story の❶～❼の文中にある空所に適切な単語を書き入れましょう。音声は２回繰り返されます。　CD 29

● News Story

Narrator: Twice a month, employees of the Nagamare Kaikyo Train Line change **hats**, going from railroad conductors to tour operators. ❶ They turn a regular train into a sightseeing cruiser, altering the layout and putting up decorations, (　　　[1]) (　　　[2]) (　　　[3]) (　　　[4]) (　　　[5]) (　　　[6]).

❶ その多くは自分たちで買った

Sightseeing trains in Japan run the **gamut** in price. For example, this ultra-luxury sleeper train cost about 90 million dollars to build.

On the other hand, remodeling the Nagamare Kaikyo cost about 90 thousand dollars. Despite the bargain basement budget, it won the grand prize last year in a contest for Japanese railroad tours.

Man: There's a squid.

Girl: It's like being in the ocean.

Narrator: Starting from Hakodate Station, the route takes passengers on a four-hour, round-trip ride along the coast of Hokkaido. Two years ago, a **semipublic** railway company **took over** the train line. But **budget projections** suggested continuing **shortfalls** for the coming decade. ❷ To **lure** more customers, the firm (　　　[1]) (　　　[2]) (　　　[3]) (　　　[4]) (　　　[5]) (　　　[6]).

❷ 観光列車を走らせることを決めた

***Yasuo Katsumata** (Sales section manager, South Hokkaido Railway Company):* ❸ The train line can't survive (　　　[1]) (　　　[2]) (　　　[3]) (　　　[4]) (　　　[5]) (　　　[6]), so we thought we should try something new. We started offering people sightseeing packages that are very attractive.

❸ 私たちが観光事業で集客をしなければ

Narrator: One problem was the lack of major tourist spots along the route. So the company **enlisted** the help of community members. They include Akihito Shimotomai, a local baker.

***Akihito Shimotomai* (President, Vauban bake):** Here you go! This is *bekomochi*.

Narrator: He offers visitors a treat made from rice flour and sweet bean jam. On days of the tour he has to take an extra two hours to make the *bekomochi*.

Shimotomai: ❹ As a business, it's not profitable at all, but ([1]) ([2]) ([3]) ([4]) ([5]) ([6]).

❹ 私はこれを観光客のためにやっています

Narrator: Shimotomai waits on the platform for the train to arrive and welcomes passengers in traditional station vendor style.

Later in the day, community members also lend a hand, preparing a barbecue of regional seafood.

Vendor: Here you go.

Customer: It's delicious.

Narrator: As the trip **draws to a close**, riders are treated to one more local charm, the lamps of **squid fishing boats** lighting up the night sky. ❺ The ([1]) ([2]) ([3]) ([4]) ([5]) ([6]).

❺ ツアーは成功している

❻ The Nagamare Kaikyo may hold the title of poorest sightseeing train in Japan, but it's ([1]) ([2]) ([3]) ([4]) ([5]) ([6]). ❼ It serves as an example for other rural areas and as ([1]) ([2]) ([3]) ([4]) ([5]) ([6]).

❻ 地域の魅力と思いやりでいっぱいである

❼ お金がすべてではないことを思い出させるもの

Review the Key Expressions

各問、選択肢から適切な単語を選び、英文を完成させましょう。なお、余分な単語が 1 語ずつあります。

1. 父が退職したら、私は父の会社を引き継ぐ予定だ。

I am (   ) to (   ) (   ) my (   ) company after (   ) (   ).

over take part retires going he father's

2. 手伝ってくれるなら、部室の掃除がはるかに早く済ませられる。

If you can (   ) (   ) (   ), we could (   ) (   ) the club room (   ) faster.

much cleaning lend get hand finish a

3. (私たちの) その町での旅行が終わりに近づいたとき、私は財布が盗まれていることに気付いた。

(   ) our tour of the city (   ) (   ) a (   ), I (   ) that my wallet (   ) been stolen.

had when to discovered close drew end

4. 明確な津波避難計画を立てるのに、この悲劇が後世に伝えるものとして役に立たなければならない。

This (   ) must (   ) (   ) a reminder to future (   ) to have clear tsunami (   ) plans in place.

evacuation serve tragedy vacancy generations as

● Discussion Questions

1. Are you interested in the Nagamare Kaikyo sightseeing train? Why or why not?

2. If you travel abroad, what would you like to see or do? Why?

UNIT 15

Friendship Voyage

日米の「絆」
―― 震災をきっかけに

青森県八戸市にある厳島神社の鳥居上部が東日本大震災の津波で流失し、２年後に米国西海岸のオレゴン州に漂着した。後にその笠木（かさぎ）は日本に返却され、鳥居が再建された。これをきっかけに、子どもたちが友好関係を築こうとお互いに 7,000km も離れたオレゴン州と青森県で、ある実験をすることにした。

● Words & Phrases

CD 30

- □ **vessel**　船〈ship や boat より堅い言い方〉
- □ **current**　海流
  The boat turned over and the people drowned due to the heavy *current*.
  ボートが転覆し、強い海流のため人々はおぼれた。
- □ **figurehead**　船首像
- □ to **mean**　～の意味をもつ、重要性をもつ
  Money *means* everything to him.
  彼にとってはお金がすべてだ。
- □ to **initiate**　〈計画、事業など〉を始める
- □ **bow**　船首
- □ to **make it**　《口語》（うまく）たどり着く
- □ **release**　解放〈ここでは、船を水面におろすこと〉

Before You Watch

以下は、人々などの「関係」に関する記述です。下の枠内から適切な単語を選び、空所に入れましょう。

1. その両国の関係は強固なままである。
( ) between the two countries ( ) strong.

2. どこの（地域）社会に属していても、人間関係はもっとも重要だ。
No ( ) what community you're in, ( ) relationships are the most important thing.

3. 事業で成功するには、十分な社交性が大切だ。
It is important to have good social ( ) to be successful in business.

4. 彼はちょっとした知り合いだ。 He is a casual ( ).

5. 彼女は恋人ではなくてただの友達だ。 She is not my ( ), just a friend.

6. 彼らは三角関係にある。 They are in a love-( ) relationship.

7. 私たちは仕事仲間です。 We are business ( ).

8. 多くの人が職場でのいじめや人間関係に悩んでいる。
Many people are troubled by ( ) and bad relationships in the workplace.

9. 私たちは遠距離恋愛の関係だ。 We are in a ( )-distance relationship.

10. 彼らはお互いにさらに深く関わっている。
They ( ) with each other on a deeper level.

acquaintance	bullying	connect	girlfriend	long	matter
partners	personal	relations	remain	skills	triangle

Watch the News

First Viewing

ニュースを見て、内容と合っているものはT、違っているものはFを選びましょう。

1. These boats were designed to sail across the Atlantic Ocean. [T / F]

2. The boats are equipped with devices for global positioning. [T / F]

3. The project was started by a mayor in Oregon. [T / F]

Understand the News　Second Viewing

1 ニュースをもう一度見て、各問の空所に入る適切な選択肢を a 〜 c から選びましょう。

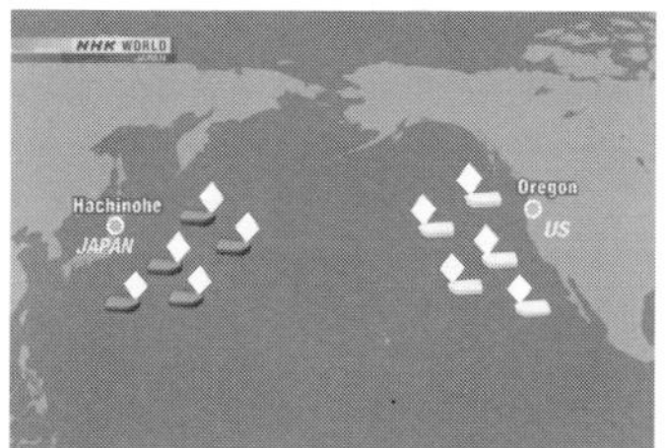

1. The experiment is designed to find out if ____.
- **a.** pollution of the sea is a serious and urgent global problem
- **b.** the GPS device functions well under any weather conditions
- **c.** the current will carry the boats to the other side of the ocean

2. These students in Aomori ____.
- **a.** visited Oregon on a cultural exchange program
- **b.** have not met the students in Oregon
- **c.** have the know-how to make small boats

3. Sandel says that ____.
- **a.** children remember feelings and relationships
- **b.** the sciences are important subjects in school
- **c.** Japanese school kids should learn how to communicate in English

2 右の文字列を並べ替えて単語を作り、各文の空所に入れて意味がとおるようにしましょう。語頭の文字（群）が与えてあるものもあります。

1. A long journey in a ship is called a (　　　　　　　　).　[eagoyv]
2. Children from both Oregon and Aomori feel a (**c**　　　　　　　　).　[oncontine]
3. Sandel wants to start long-lasting (　　　　　　　　) among the kids. 〈複数形〉　[shendipfris]
4. The boats were carried by fishermen for (**re**　　　　　　　　) on the open sea.　[leesa]

3 CD の音声を聞いて、次ページ News Story の❶〜❼の文中にある空所に適切な単語を書き入れましょう。音声は２回繰り返されます。　CD 31

● News Story

Anchor: The red *torii* gates in Japan's northern prefecture of Aomori are a defining feature of the region. The originals were destroyed by the tsunami in 2011. Parts of them drifted across the Pacific and were found on the west coast of Oregon. ❶ Thanks to a cross-continent effort, (　　　[1]) (　　　[2]) (　　　[3]) (　　　[4]) (　　　[5]) (　　　[6]). But that was just the beginning. NHK World's Yuuka Ogawa reports on a project that has kids in Japan and the U.S. working together.

❶（漂着した）部分は返還され修復された

Narrator: Students in Oregon put together glass fiber boats and prepared them for a long voyage. ❷ The two-meter-long **vessels** were made for launching into the Pacific in hopes they (　　　[1]) (　　　[2]) (　　　[3]) (　　　[4]) (　　　[5]) (　　　[6]).

❷ 日本に向かって進む

Five boats were to set sail from Oregon, another five to be released from Hachinohe. Students will see if **currents** will carry them to the other side of the Pacific, just like the *torii*. ❸ The boats are equipped with GPS devices (　　　[1]) (　　　[2]) (　　　[3]) (　　　[4]) (　　　[5]) (　　　[6]). This team decided to install a *torii* gate as a **figurehead**. The members learned how much it would **mean** to kids in Hachinohe.

❸ どこまで進んだかわかる［跡をたどれる］ように

Leah Paris: Well, I think they're going to be surprised and happy because we, uh, we have a connection...

Narrator: An educator from Oregon **initiated** the project. Nate Sandel visited Hachinohe late last year and met local children. He had heard much about the *torii* before making the journey.

***Nate Sandel* (Education Director, Columbia River Maritime Museum):** (*He points at one of the torii gates.*) Ah, and this is, this is the one from Oregon? Oregon brought that? (*He talks to a girl student.*) And do you remember when they brought it back?

Ami Shinnumadate: Yes, I was very happy.

Sandel: Yeah. This is it! This is the connection between Oregon and Aomori.

Narrator: Sandel brought the boats from the U.S.

Sandel: ❹ The students ([1]) ([2]) ([3]) ([4]) ([5]) ([6]).

❹ みなさんのために特別な贈り物を作った

Narrator: The *torii* gate on the **bow** came as a surprise, made by friends they had not yet met.

Rio Shinnumadate: Amazing!

Rina Takashimizu: I felt a real connection to them.

Narrator: ❺ ([1]) ([2]) ([3]) ([4]) ([5]) ([6]) and drew a *torii* gate on the sail. ❻ They ([1]) ([2]) ([3]) ([4]) ([5]).

❺ 日本の子どもたちが飾りをつけた

❻ メッセージつきの自画像も描いた［含めた］

Haru Takahashi: I wrote, "I want us to be friends." I hope our boats **make it** to Oregon.

Sandel: ... create sort of a lasting friendship. That's really what my main hope is. You know, science and all that stuff, that's part of the school, but the friendship and the emotional, ... that's, that's the extra, and that's what I think the kids will remember the most.

Narrator: The boats are now ready. Students carried them carefully, wishing them safe travels.

Fishermen carried the vessels to the open sea for **release**.

All children: Good luck!

Narrator: Children on both sides of the ocean are tracking the crossing and exchanging updates. ❼ ([1]) ([2]) ([3]) ([4]) ([5]) ([6]) across the Pacific. Yuuka Ogawa, NHK World, Hachinohe.

❼ 彼らの希望と夢が船旅をする

Review the Key Expressions

各問、選択肢から適切な単語を選び、英文を完成させましょう。なお、余分な単語が 1 語ずつあります。

1. この棚を組み立てるのを手伝ってくれない。何か部品が不足しているのかな。

Could you come and ( ) me ( ) this shelf ( )? I'm ( ) ( ) some pieces are ( ).

if help together losing missing wondering put

2. そのシカゴ行きの飛行機は、私たちが空港に着くまでにすでに離陸していた。

The plane to Chicago ( ) already ( ) ( ) by the ( ) we ( ) ( ) the airport.

to had taken time off got touched

3. それらのテレビタレントが暴力団と関わっていた。そのスキャンダルはファンにとってまったくの驚きだった。

Those TV ( ) were ( ) ( ) a gang. The scandal ( ) ( ) a complete ( ) to their fans.

surprise participated involved personalities as with came

4. いつも使う電車路線で事故があった。（それで）ふだんより 1 時間も遅くようやく職場に着いた。

There was an ( ) on the ( ) line I always use. I finally ( ) ( ) to my ( ) one hour later than ( ).

railroad usual it accident made office reached

● Discussion Questions

1. What extracurricular activity do you remember most during your years at school?

2. If you were an organizer of an international friendship program for children, what project would you like to work on?

このテキストのメインページ
www.kinsei-do.co.jp/plusmedia/40

次のページの QR コードを読み取る
直接ページにジャンプできます

オンライン映像配信サービス「plus⁺Media」について

本テキストの映像は plus⁺Media ページ（www.kinsei-do.co.jp/plusmedia）から、ストリーミング再生でご利用いただけます。手順は以下に従ってください。

ログイン

ログインページ

●ご利用には、ログインが必要です。
サイトのログインページ（www.kinsei-do.co.jp/plusmedia/login）へ行き、plus⁺Media パスワード（次のページのシールをはがしたあとに印字されている数字とアルファベット）を入力します。

●パスワードは各テキストにつき１つです。
有効期限は、はじめてログインした時点から１年間になります。

[利用方法]

次のページにある QR コード、もしくは plus⁺Media トップページ（www.kinsei-do.co.jp/plusmedia）から該当するテキストを選んで、そのテキストのメインページにジャンプしてください。

メニューページ　　再生画面

plus+Media トップ　　メインページ

「Video」「Audio」をタッチすると、それぞれのメニューページにジャンプしますので、そこから該当する項目を選べば、ストリーミングが開始されます。

[推奨環境]

iOS (iPhone, iPad)	OS: iOS 6～13 ブラウザ：標準ブラウザ	Android	OS: Android 4.x～9.0 ブラウザ：標準ブラウザ、Chrome
PC	OS: Windows 7/8/8.1/10, MacOS X　ブラウザ: Internet Explorer 10/11, Microsoft Edge, Firefox 48以降, Chrome 53以降, Safari		

※最新の推奨環境についてはウェブサイトをご確認ください。
※上記の推奨環境を満たしている場合でも、機種によってはご利用いただけない場合もあります。また、推奨環境は技術動向等により変更される場合があります。予めご了承ください。

本書には音声 CD（別売）があります

NHK NEWSLINE 3

映像で学ぶ NHK 英語ニュースが伝える日本 3

2020年 1 月20日　初版第 1 刷発行
2022年 4 月10日　初版第 5 刷発行

編著者　山﨑達朗
Stella M. Yamazaki

発行者　福岡正人

発行所　株式会社　金星堂

（〒101-0051）東京都千代田区神田神保町 3-21

Tel. (03) 3263-3828（営業部）

(03) 3263-3997（編集部）

Fax (03) 3263-0716

http://www.kinsei-do.co.jp

編集担当　西田　碧　　Printed in Japan

印刷所・製本所／大日本印刷株式会社

ISBN978-4-7647-4095-2 C1082